SASQUATCH
SHAMAN OF THE WOODS

RUSSELL WIITALA

Copyright © 2021 by Russell Wiitala.

ISBN 978-1-956691-01-6 (softcover)
ISBN 978-1-956691-02-3 (hardcover)
ISBN 978-1-956691-00-9 (ebook)
Library of Congress Control Number: 2021922178

All rights reserved. No part of this book may be reproduced or transmitted in any form or by any means, electronic or mechanical, including photocopying, recording, or by any information storage and retrieval system without express written permission from the author, except in the case of brief quotations embodied in critical reviews and certain other noncommercial uses permitted by copyright law.

Printed in the United States of America.

Orion Press
www.orionpressbooks.com
1382 Belmont Road, Raymond, WA 98577

CONTENTS

Foreword 5

Chapter 1: 50/50 9

Chapter 2: Now What? 25

Chapter 3: Time to Expand 36

Chapter 4: The Playhouse 62

Chapter 5: The Woo 71

Chapter 6: My Awakening 85

Chapter 7: Bringing Family 96

Chapter 8: Montana House of Mystery 115

Chapter 9: Synchronicities 135

Chapter 10: Home Is Where The Heart Is 141

Chapter 11: Nicola Tesla 162

Chapter 12: What is Going On? 174

FOREWORD

When I relate my experiences to my friends and family they listen politely and sometimes enthusiastically. I also see an occasional wink and smirk. I try and not let it bother me too much, because there was a day when I would have done the same. I have had many different adventures in my life. At a wedding dinner once, a question came up during a game they played? The question was "Who in the family is most likely to be a spy?" Everyone in the family picked me without hesitation. Much of the time, they never know where I am or what I am doing? I have been somewhat of an enigma for my extended family. A ghostly figure who comes and haunts the family get-togethers on occasion.

Within my extended family I have a reputation for being a good raconteur. The children in the family request my stories with enthusiasm, especially ones about my big forest friends, the sasquatch. At my cousins cabin the kids have a story staff they bring me when it is time for another story. We then go to a special place in the woods for storytelling. I'm glad to give them every detail. I consider them my most important audience. Some of the adults, when I'm not around, tell the children they are just stories. I always try and remember to correct the record on that before I relate one of my latest adventures. The reason the stories flow so well is because I have actually experienced them. I'm not so confident that I remember every detail accurately, but the events did occur and I've related them many times over the last few years to many people as accurately as I remember them. The stories can be quite bizarre. Fortunately, I do have witnesses for many of them. Otherwise, I might come to the conclusion that I'm hallucinating or even insane.

Storytelling to a small audience is my favorite way to relate what I've experienced and learned. I have eye contact and can answer any question the listener might have?

I'd rather not write this book, except as a personal recollection for myself and my family. I've written this book and am going to publish because I believe it is my duty. You'll understand, better once you've read it. The sharing of knowledge is important, no matter how it might originally be accepted? This book might serve as a guide for someone who follows? I learned much from reading the technical books on sasquatch and even more from reading reported encounters. I always listen carefully to anyone who bothers to share their knowledge with me as experiencers. We are linked in an important chain that is advancing our understanding one event at a time. Each link, no matter how humble, is important. That is how knowledge is collected, enhanced and forwarded.

After my realization that sasquatch do exist, I originally thought I'd just go out and hangout with these mysterious beings by playing a little music and camping out once in a while. I thought we would just be friends for the rest of my life. Sure, I'd read and heard about metaphysical occurrences being linked to sasquatch, but I really didn't know what to make of those "Woo" stories? I am glad that I did not dismiss them outright. My original plan took an oblique turn that became a complete surprise when I was taken for a deep dive into the rabbit hole.

Sasquatch Shaman of the Woods

CHAPTER 1

50/50

I'VE ALWAYS BEEN curious about esoteric, mystical and deep philosophical subjects. I remember, as a boy, trying to engage my friends in such conversation only to be disappointed with their passive participation and blank stares. They had never considered such nonsense and were more interested in making better use of our time on the ball field.

I wanted to know about the universe and how it worked? My boyhood buddies already knew it worked in accordance with our accepted cultural belief system and no questions were necessary or wanted.

I was taught at a young age that it was cultural taboo to believe inanimate objects hold mystical powers. Ghosts, telepathy, ET's, bigfoot, fairies and so on are all considered figments of the human imagination to those who conform to modern western culture. Shamans, according to this belief system, work with the human psyche, the placebo effect and nothing more.

When I was a young lad, I was very fond of science fiction movies such as The Day the Earth Stood Still and television shows such as The Twilight Zone, Outer Limits and Star Trek. It made me wonder what strange things might be lurking in our universe? It was a huge universe after all. How big? I read somewhere that if you crunched the universe into the size of the American continent, the earth would be so small you couldn't detect it with an electron microscope. Considering the size, why would our tiny and insignificant planet be the only one to harbor life in this vast universe?

Most humans are too comfortably ensconced within concrete jungles and the framework of modern society to consider such a question? Many of are too busy and too absorbed to consider anything beyond pop culture and trying to earn a living. Others are too afraid to think of anything other than the reality they've been taught to believe in.

Fear can control humans very effectively. Most don't even realize that a chuckle over something they consider as an absurd idea might be just whistling through the cemetery. A quick laugh is a way to shut the door on something they find uncomfortable. In many cases making light of something not understood or believed is an attempt to quickly dismiss an unacceptable, possible alternative reality. Very effective for the person to ridicule and dismiss, lest the fear seeps in.

I was never a committed believer or nonbeliever of ghosts, UFO's and bigfoot. Over the years my beliefs have waffled back and forth across the fence, before settling, once again, on top of it. I always wanted to know the objective truth and there wasn't enough evidence to convince me to get off of that fence and commit to anything. How does our universe really work? Are there other worlds like ours? Are ghosts real? Do portals, other dimensions and parallel universes exist? Is an expiration date for Twinkies necessary? I found thinking and researching these strange concepts captivating, with the exception of bigfoot and Twinkies, which I never thought much about.

Knowing what I know now, I wonder why I never thought about bigfoot? I now know, for instance that I had what I believe was my first encounter with a forest person around 1982, while fishing cut-throat trout.

Cut throat trout are sea going trout that migrate back up the rivers and creeks to spawn. Just like steelhead and salmon they return to the same water where they were born to conceive the next generation. When the cut-throats were running, I'd go out one or two times a week and catch my dinner. Usually, it didn't take long for me to return with a fish for a meal. I had a place where I could ascend down a steep grade onto the banks of Smith creek, just above tide water. Then I'd fish my way up the river to my favorite fishing hole, where I would also camp overnight once in a while. One day, as I was fishing, I kept hearing rocks come off the ridge line way above me. Occasionally, depending on where you are, rocks will come off cliffs and cascade down in that deep cut valley. But I wasn't in an area where rocks sluff that often. Also, the sound of the rocks shadowed me as I fished my way up stream. I wondered if it was a bear? Was a bear kicking rocks? I wondered why a bear would move parallel to me in that manner and what is up with the rocks!? What else could it be than a bear? I knew it wasn't a cougar, because a cougar follows from behind and is silent. It was so puzzling I never forgot it.

This happened a long time ago, so I can't remember every detail. I do remember the rocks, because it made no sense to me? A human couldn't have traversed those gnarly ridges to keep up with me, so I dismissed the thought that someone was playing me. It wasn't until I started studying testimonials and having my own encounters with forest people that I realized it must have been a bigfoot tossing those rocks. Perhaps, that was a gentle wake-up call, a sort of subtle first call from the wild. A tap on the shoulder is how my friend, Joe Hauser, puts it.

If, at the time, science accepted bigfoot as being real I would have considered that being a possible source of the rocks. In my mind bigfoot was a probable myth and therefore not worthy of consideration as a possible source of cascading rocks. At the time I knew nothing of sasquatch's habit of tossing rocks. In fact, I knew practically nothing about bigfoot, period.

I had also experienced the metaphysical from a young age, yet I denied it. When I was eleven, I had a premonition that a shirt tail cousin, whom I loved and considered my uncle, was going to die. I also knew the cause of death about a year before he died. He would die at a steel plant when a crane cut a live electrical line causing it to wrap around his body. I did have the premonition that it would be by an electrified line, but nothing more. I didn't tell anyone at the time, because I had been taught that premonitions don't exist. I had convinced myself that the premonition must not be true. After he died, I didn't tell a soul about my premonition for years. From that experience I learned that pre-cognition exists, possibly? Until I had another one about fifteen years later in my late twenties, I still held doubt.

When I was in my late twenties, while living with my parents for a short time, I had come home to nap in the early afternoon after work. I dreamt I saw the sod catch fire from my folks burn pile and burn underground until it went up an alder tree. When I woke up, I told my mother about the dream, since it seemed so real and bizarre. About three hours later mom came in and asked me to come with her. She had started the burn pile and the sod did catch on fire and had worked its way underground to the base of an alder tree about thirty feet away. I believe it was burning an old rotted root from a hemlock that had been dropped years before. The alder was the tree in my dream. So, I saw exactly what would happen.

After that event I began reading about the occult. I now knew that pre-cognition was real. I wondered what else could be real? Telepathy? Telekinesis?

I admit that I was always a skeptic about religion. I was a show me guy, not a tell me guy. I noticed that the same people telling me I should believe in God had their own subjective beliefs about other subjects that I thought were erroneous, or at the very least, questionable. People seemed to be subject to their own prejudices. So why should I believe them when they tell me who or what God is? Or even if God exists? Why so many different religions and different creation stories? Why were there so many contradictory beliefs and every congregation had their own idea about how to worship God? I thought, if there are different interpretations, how can you call it an objective belief? When I was very young, I didn't know the word objective, but I certainly understood the principle. I wanted to know for sure what to believe. I didn't want anyone telling me what I should believe. I'm still that way, by the way.

When I was quite young, I remember sitting in Sunday school looking around and wondering if I was the only one there with doubts? It was a lonely feeling and I kept it to myself.

Yet at times, I admit I felt a little superior to others. I believed I was more objective than most human beings. I also realized how tricky the human brain is and that maybe I was fooling myself?

I came across a study that tested people on their ability to discern objective fact verse subjective opinion. I was surprised how many people couldn't tell the difference between opinion and objective fact. Some opinions, depending on the individual's leanings, were considered cold hard fact and some cold hard facts were considered opinion. How could that be? I took the test to see if I could tell the difference between fact or opinion and I scored 100% in knowing the difference. Yet, 75% of the population have trouble with that test. I could easily tell the difference between empirical fact and opinion. It was like being tested on what an A is as opposed to a B. It seemed very simple and elementary to me. It appears I'm in the minority. Ultimately, that did not surprise me and confirmed what I've believed my whole life.

Recently, I saw a picture of a UFO on a news feed. It's hard to tell what it was, but it really looked strange. The text on the picture read "I hate to break it to you, but there has never been any evidence to support our being visited by ET's." Never? Really? Is that a factual statement or an opinion? It's an opinion of course. There are all kinds of evidence that we are being visited in the form of eye witness testimony, photos, official historical documents, video and even strange alloys detected in metals recovered and claimed to be from ET aircraft. That reporter has the right to reject all evidence on UFOs, but it is his subjective opinion and not an objective fact that all of the evidence is total bunk.

There have been chunks of metal alloys that have been retrieved by eye witnesses who saw them drip from UFO's. In other cases, people have come into possession of metal by other means, such as through metal detection of suspected crash sites. Expert metallurgists who have examined these objects have said that some of these metals are extremely unusual and that, in some cases, they wouldn't know how to produce such an alloy or material? That is a true mystery, isn't it? What about all the eye witnesses, pictures and videos? Is that evidence? Of course, it is. How could that reporter dismiss that outright? That reporter found a way and many who read his report would consider his opinion, fact. He does not agree that witness testimony and photographic evidence is evidence. That, again, is his opinion and not fact. Yet many will believe he is stating fact. That human quirk of subjectivity complicates everything.

Late in 2019, the Navy released some video shot from the gun camera of a F-18. One set of pilots that encountered these UAPs (unidentified aerial phenomenon) as the military now calls them, described them as being shaped like a Tic-tac. A Navy radar tracked one UAP diving straight down from 28,000 feet to 50 feet above the ocean surface in less than a second. They calculated a speed of 20,000 miles per hour during the descent, before it came to a dead stop and hover just fifty feet over the surface of the Pacific Ocean. The "tic tacks" were obviously intelligently operated judging by their playful maneuvers with the F-18s. I believe the Navy, in releasing these videos, released some very substantial evidence.

Recently, more people are beginning to believe that UFOs are real. They are starting to pay attention and not as many are laughing anymore. They are being helped with some interesting reveals by the government.

The human brain is as mysterious as the rest of the universe. Advances in understanding the way it works have progressed considerably, but have a long way to go. I believe my brain is a little different than most. For instance, I took six vacations in Vegas and paid for five of them from my winnings. How did I do that? I was more objective with my approach to gambling. I never made a sucker bet. I always play the games with the best pay off and so on. Why don't more tourists do that? Vegas would have to scramble to tighten everything up. Then I couldn't win there anymore, not that I'm ever going back there again. I only visited because my niece and her family lived there for a while. My consistent luck in Vegas and other personal quirks tell me that my brain is built just a little different than most.

Is it superior? No, just different. I have difficulty in social situations. I pretty much understand people, I just don't know how to deal with them very well. In certain familiar places I'm fine. For instance, I've spent thirty-five plus years in the local playhouse. In the playhouse I'm not bad, so I like it there. I feel like I can be myself while not being myself. At my home I'm almost normal. My family and most of my cousins are very comfortable with my quirks. Some see my, so called, contact with sasquatch as sort of a fantasy in my brain. Some harmless misinterpretations of otherwise explainable occurrences. However, some family members have seen and or heard amazing things while they were with me out in the wild. Because of that, not as many of my family members roll their eyes and chuckle when I tell a story anymore.

A while ago a friend was telling me about an illness our mutual friend's husband was suffering from. She told me that doctors had finally figured out what his problem was. As she was telling me the diagnosis, she hesitated as she struggled with the name of the ailment. I finished her sentence for her and said "Crohn's disease." She asked, "How did you know that!? It took the doctors two years to figure that out!" I had seen a few postings on Facebook by our mutual friend and came to the conclusion that it was probably Crohn's disease. To me, it seemed an obvious possibility? This puzzles me? Why did it take so long for the experts to come to the same conclusion? I hardly know her husband. I played with him at a couple of open mics years ago and that is it. A few postings with some testimonials were all it took and I'd come to an accurate diagnosis, unless the doctors are wrong?

Through the years I've experienced this, many times. I appear to have a knack for coming up with the correct answer when given minimal data. I have not always been correct in my assessments, But I do believe my batting average is way better than most. It could be that I have a touch of Asperger's syndrome? I've thought it might be the case for years. One day, a friend of mine, who has a degree in psychology and a mother with the condition said "You know you have Asperger's don't you?" That was enough confirmation for me. I really don't need to go in and get tested. I'm doing fine with whatever this is? In fact, I consider it my super power and I utilized that term long before I heard Greta Thornburg use it. If I do have it, it is a very mild case and could account for my ability to win in Vegas, as well as other quirks I exhibit?

In my late twenties I had moved to Raymond Washington. I decided to make a concerted effort to find religion. Living in a conservative community I saw it as a way to integrate with the "normal humans". I say normal, because I've always felt like I had to struggle to fit in with the rest of humanity. I always felt I was on the outside looking in and not really understanding? Could that be because of Asperger's? So, I read the bible cover to cover, went to bible class and had a lot of questions about the contradictions I noticed. When the bible teacher brought up something I would ask "But what about where it says this?" After listening to her explain away in a very convoluted and obviously subjective manner I gave up and left the class for good. Later a friend who was in that class, told me that when I left the bible teacher expressed how relieved she was. The teacher said she always felt the presence of the devil when I was there. Was that her objective analysis at work? All I was doing was asking questions. Are questions forbidden? Oops, that's a question.

I also studied other religions and philosophy in a search for answers. I certainly wouldn't consider myself a scholar on religion though, just a casual browser. I concluded there was wisdom in all the religions I studied. There is also a lot of strange and wonderous stories within religious myth. However, I was not convinced by anything I read that God existed or that any of the wild myths within any religion could be true. The imagery and apparent contradiction to Newtonian physics told me not to take them too seriously.

I did read Chariots of Fire by Erich Von Daniken in the seventies. That book questioned ancient history and our interpretations of the bible. At the time I was underwhelmed. All of his questions seemed way too farfetched to be taken seriously. Yet, the imagery of the bible makes much more sense if you apply the questions in Von Daniken's book to it. My personal question would be, how might ancient people describe a UFO or an ET if they saw one? Might they describe a flying saucer as a chariot of fire with wheels within wheels? To me, that seems a likely description by those who lived in our distant past, if they witnessed such a flying machine? It should make you wonder if ET's might have been the inspiration for a few of those ancient bible stories?

What I find interesting is to look back on my life and realize I was subject to the same western culture of denial that has made people reject the notion of spirits, other realms of reality, portals and any forms of metaphysics for centuries. There has been a power struggle over belief systems going on for several millennia. Those with the most power have their version of the truth integrated with society and all rivals are liars, crazy or in concert with nefarious forces which must be stamped out. So, they start an inquisition and burn witches at the stake and so on…

Around the year 400, the roman emperor, Theodosius, declared all paganism and beliefs in metaphysics illegal and it stuck. If you did practice or believe in metaphysics you would be converted, tortured or executed, if you were caught. So, people became careful about who they shared their metaphysical experiences and ideas with. That spurred the creation of several secret societies and covens.

Over centuries this agenda, like a latent hangover, has controlled much of modern civilization and even our individual subconscious. The old ways of the shaman and metaphysics were discarded and replaced by our major modern organized religions, at least in most of the so-called civilized world.

In fact, we really don't have a common belief system. All of the power struggles between the religions and denominations demonstrate that on a daily basis. Humans, in the long run, are like herding cats. What we do have is a very popular western culture of metaphysical denial, shared by many of the participants of major religions and atheists alike. When I was a kid, I thought that shaman or "medicine men", were a little humorous the way they generally characterized them in movies. I believed such superstitions were not to be taken seriously in this modern day and age.

Eventually, the reductionist in me turned to quantum physics. Why wouldn't the real truth be revealed within objective science? It turns out that science isn't completely objective either. An experiment, especially a weird one, such as the double slot experiment is wide open to interpretation. What does it mean when it gives one kind of result if the experimenter is observing the experiment and another when he isn't observing it? We don't know and that intrigues me. I viewed quantum physics as very strange and wonderous. It is different from religion in that the theories can be tested, to a degree. It has an almost objective approach to the mysteries of our universe, yet is still open to wild interpretation. How fun!

For those uninitiated to the double slit experiment, I will give a brief explanation. While shooting a single photon (unit of light in quantum physics) at two slits, the photon will go through one or the other, if it is being observed by the experimenter. If the experimenter doesn't watch, the photon appears to become a wave and go through both slits simultaneously. The wave pattern is recorded and indicates that the photon acted like a wave when not observed. The wave pattern represents all possible routes for the individual photon. Does this illustrate how all of reality works, or just how it works on the sub atomic level? Recently, I've read that they do believe it's possible the results in quantum experiments could reflect our world on a macro level. If that is the case, then we manifest our reality as we observe it. Try and wrap your head around that one.

Do we participate in the making of our universe? Are we all god like? When a tree falls in the woods without anyone there, does it really happen?

Eventually, in my forties, I jumped off the agnostic fence and started thinking of myself as an atheist/nonspiritual skeptic. I decided that I would still keep an open mind to any evidence or testimonial, but not so much that my brains would fall out. I believed sincerely at the time I was unlikely to ever change my self-proclaimed status.

My early attraction to UFO's, ghosts and general weirdness never left me. There was a lot of contemporary evidence to consider. There continued to be an accumulation of photos and other evidence gathered about UFOs. There were even those who claimed they had been abducted. Is everyone who claim to have contact lying, mistaken or delusional? There seemed to be so many testimonials with a common thread, that it appeared to me unlikely that everyone could be lying or delusional. Was there a quirk in our human brains that made us see things or believe things that weren't real? Do ETs really exist? I came to believe these were the right questions to satisfy my curiosity, if they were ever answered. Questions that might be, at least partially, answered within my lifetime.

There were other mysteries to contemplate as well. I was fifteen when I saw an article in Argosy magazine that caught my attention for a brief moment. It was an article documenting the filming of a, so called, bigfoot. In October of 1967, the time of the Patterson/Gimlin filming, I was living in Grants Pass Oregon, not far away from Bluff Creek in northern California where they claimed the film was made.

Is bigfoot real? That question faded with time. I heard a couple of curious local stories, after moving to Raymond Washington, but I didn't give them much thought. Then, as fate would have it, I took a walk with my friend Russell Wilson and suddenly the question of bigfoot sprung to life.

It was just days after my retirement from the postal service in May of 2007 when Russell Wilson and I took a walk. He asked me if I'd heard about the local family that saw a bigfoot while out hiking? I responded by saying "Whaaat!?" Then, impulsively, I asked, "Do you want to go looking for bigfoot?" He, being a somewhat impulsive person, replied "YES!"

It was the perfect moment for such an adventure. I had just retired and wanted to re-connect with the wilderness. I used to hunt and fish, but quit and took up golf, flying, acting, directing, snow skiing and also did a lot of water skiing. My time in the wilderness had become little more than an annual camping trip. At the time of my retirement, I still had an airplane, but my other activities had dwindled to just the theater and snow skiing. I felt I had all of this new-found time on my hands and this was a perfect activity for getting back to the wilderness. I told Russell up front that I'd give bigfoot a 50/50 chance of existence. We'd go out looking and I'd begin to study the subject and we would see what we could find?

I really thought, in my naivete, that if they were out there, I would find them. I would use my super power. I figured I'd read up about them and then go out there and track them down in no time, if they really exist? It turned out not to be so easy. As I read testimonials and listened to recordings of calls and viewed film and photos, I became more convinced that there might be something to it. There couldn't possibly be thousands of hoaxers out there making all of those prints, costumes and such. Especially prints that had been examined by experts and couldn't be easily dismissed as fake. Some of the prints had visible dermal ridges, for instance. How would someone fake that? Especially since they seemed unique and consistent across the continent, according to primate print experts.

Besides going out and looking for evidence I conducted my own survey by asking everyone I knew and sometimes even strangers if they had seen, heard, or knew of anyone who had an encounter? It turned out, in my home town, that about one in fifteen or so either knew someone who had an experience that they thought was bigfoot, or they themselves had an experience. A few of these people actually saw one. Only one person I talked to had reported her incident. That meant that encounters were grossly under reported. I still hear these reports on a regular basis from those who know me and know what I do. The last one reported to me was a sighting of one running across a road just outside of town just a few weeks before this writing.

After four years of searching high and low and every nasty, gnarly corner of the county Russell and I had only found one possible foot print. What were we doing wrong? I was hearing eye witness testimony about them locally and yet I couldn't find them? I was beginning to think it was time to give up. Maybe, my so-called super power wasn't up to it?

I had hiked the trail at least a couple of hundred times where Russell told me the family claimed to have seen a bigfoot. I had nothing to show for it, except a renewed love of the outdoors. In the spring of 2011, soon after I started thinking it was about time to give up, I had an experience on that access road. The wind was in my face as I hiked up and I smelled something I thought was a dead animal. However, I kept smelling it as I hiked higher and higher. That didn't seem right? I should have passed the carcass a half mile back? I hiked a spur on a ridge above a clear-cut and started to look for the source of the smell. I had read about bigfoot and their rancid smell, so I was on high alert. Then I heard three knocks, not far away. In fact, from where I stood, I could see the bunch of trees that lined the main road where I believed the knocks emanated from.

I built up my courage and tried to keep calm by telling myself this is what I've been looking for and then walked over to those trees. I didn't see anything, but I did get one whiff of that pungent odor again. Then I lost my nerve a bit and hiked back down the hill to my car, drove home and thought about what had just occurred.

I began to think about all the testimonials I had read and I recognized some common threads through many of them. I made a list of those commonalities. All I had to do, I figured, was go to where all those items on the list were present and they'd be there. I had already looked over hill and dale for four years so I knew the wider region very well. I picked the most likely location on Google earth and called Russell. I told him about my possible encounter and asked if he wanted to go with me to check an area out? I told him directly that I thought I could find them. Considering what little luck we had for four years it seems quite audacious that I had such returned confidence all of a sudden.

We first stopped at a landing on a ridge above the location I had chosen. Russell Wilson noticed a grubbed log that had been over turned.

I imagined it to be a bear that grubbed it. Then we noticed curious, deep, indentations where large punky logs had been. Where were the logs? Had they been thrown off of the ridge? The brush was too thick below the ridge to see if that was the case. It was obvious no equipment had been brought in to lift or drag them. Then we found a piece of punky wood that had been smashed down flat, as if stepped on by something massive. Russell, who is 6'2" and was well over 250 pounds at the time, stomped on the wood and hardly made a dent in it. There were also possible bigfoot prints to be found.

We made our way down to the landing and found nothing. When dusk came, I tried to imitate what I'd heard in recordings and screamed as loud as I could. We waited for a few minutes and then heard some twig snaps about a hundred yards below us. We could trace the progress of that something by listening to the frogs. There were a kazillion frogs spread out over the area. They would shut up when something got close, then start croaking again after that something passed. Slightly stressed, I whispered to Russell that I wasn't going to scream again. We then laughed nervously under our breath.

That was all that happened on our first trip. On our second trip I screamed and then we heard three knocks about a hundred yards down below our location. I screamed again and we heard three knocks again. Russell asked me if I was now a believer? I said I'd now give them a 65% chance of existing. That response made Russell sigh. We decided to return and camp out for a night.

Upon our return we set up camp, started a fire and settled in after dark and started to drink some beer. It was a beautiful June evening. I still wasn't convinced and looked upon our camping trip more like party time in the wilderness. After all, the movement we heard could have been an elk or bear? The knocks? Well, they were puzzling?

We joked about the shy beast coming into our camp and enjoying a beer with us. I had five beers, which is about two more than my usual upper limit and was a little tight when I went to my tent. Our tents were right next to each other after Russell Wilson had dragged his tent over next to mine, as if I was going to protect him somehow? That gave me a good laugh. We settled in and talked awhile like two boys at summer camp. Then we said our good nights and got quiet.

I took this picture of the campsite the evening of our visit.

We had been quiet for only about five minutes when I heard what sounded like pebbles hitting the ground around the tents. I listened and waited for a few minutes, then took the fatalist view that if he was going to harm us, we'd already be dead, so I drifted off to sleep. Russell on the other hand didn't sleep a wink that night.

We got up the next morning and I asked if he'd heard the pebbles and he said one hit him in the back through the tent wall. He told me that as soon as I fell asleep and started to snore something very big on two feet came into camp and stood in front of my tent for a few moments. He said he could hear his deep breathing. Then he came over to his tent and stomped next to it, as if to see if he was awake? After that he meandered around the campsite for a while before leaving. Russell was too afraid to move or fall asleep.

We started to surveil the area. Russell found a freshly grubbed tree next to the campsite and a I found a pile of vomit that matched the color of the grubbed tree. We searched every soft patch of dirt around and didn't find any prints other than elk at the edge of the landing. The landing itself is compressed gravel and not conducive to leaving much of a print, if any.

Russell asked me, again, if I was now a believer? I said "I'll raise the odds of bigfoot existence to 80 percent." Russell sighed.

Russell had already seen one up close before and knew they were real. When he was a teenager, he was driving to see a girlfriend when one came out of the underbrush, put his hand on his driver side window and then continued back into the underbrush. This happened in a suburban/rural area on a gravel road that is between Raymond and South Bend, Washington. There are old apple trees from abandoned homesteads in there and I figure he was there for a harvest.

After a few days we went back and set up camp again. We waited until dusk and I did my scream again. There were some coyotes a few hundred yards away that started to howl after my scream. After a few minutes we heard a reply scream that was very loud and sustained for about twelve seconds. At first, I thought it sounded like a souped-up four-wheel drive rig, because it began low and revved up. I began to say to Russell, "Listen to those goobers….." and that is as far as my sentence got when I realized that it was a vocal we were hearing and not a loud vehicle. When he screamed the coyote shut up! In fact, that is when the whole valley shut up! I turned to Russell and said "I'm a 110 percent believer now!" It was a total and absolute declaration of belief. He smiled in relief.

Total belief in their existence was the only option left for me at that point. I hadn't seen one yet, but instinctively I knew that no bear, elk, cougar, bobcat, coyote or anything else out there could scream that loud, or that way. It filled the valley with a primeval ambience that was profound in its gravity. It was exhilarating and satisfying at the same time. In my mind, one of those great mysteries was just solved. Bigfoot does exist and I was stoked about it!

The vocal had a human quality to it and yet I knew it couldn't be a human. It was multiple times louder and was sustained for too long. I can only manage about four seconds maximum while screaming at the top of my lungs and I am not nearly as loud. He has to have enormous lung capacity. In other words, he's big, very big!

After a few minutes we heard him move within a couple hundred yards. I asked Russell what he thought we should do? He said "I think we should get the hell out of here." So, we very hastily shoved all the camping equipment back into my Subaru and left. I really didn't think we would be harmed, but it seemed like it was the respectful thing to do at the time and I'm all about giving them respect, especially when they scream like that.

On the way back to town we decided to call him Becho, by combining the words big and echo.

CHAPTER 2

Now What?

The next time we visited the landing I set up a trail camera. We then placed a KFC chicken bucket in a limb of a tree directly across from it. How could they resist KFC, right? The only thing we ever got on the trail cam was a strange beam of light coming down from above around 2:30 a.m. in the morning. The camera was being triggered by small limbs swaying in a breeze coming from the south. The source of the light beam moved around from above as if it was trying to maneuver to get a better view of the wildlife camera. It lingered for twenty-two minutes. There was no down wash like a helicopter would cause, so what was it? Besides, why would a helicopter linger for twenty-two minutes? I doubt anyone would have been that fascinated by a trail cam? We got a good laugh over attempting to photograph bigfoot and getting a UFO instead.

Several months after that incident Russell, his ex and I were driving back from band practice in Elma Washington. I had to drop them off in Aberdeen and then drive back to my home in Raymond. As we emerged from a hail storm into a clear dark sky, a very bright light came from behind and was first visible to me on the upper right boarder of the windshield. In other words, it almost came directly over us. It was about the size of a small, single engine aircraft, but I could make out very little of any structure because it was so bright. I was in the middle of a sentence about music when I changed course and asked "What the F#$% is that!?

The light was oval shaped. It was moving at several hundred miles per hour angling slightly away from the freeway with no sound. Then it made a rising fifteen-degree right turn, climbed a few hundred feet and then turned very quickly back to the left at about seventy degrees before crossing over the freeway in front of us by less than a half mile. At that point I would estimate it to be around 2500 feet above the ground. It then slowed down and paralleled the freeway for seven to nine minutes as it outpaced us slightly. At one point it looked to me as if it was hovering, but that was not Russell Wilson's impression. We finally lost it behind some trees for a couple of minutes and it was gone when we emerged where we could see it again, had it still been there.

At the time, I knew nothing of the UFO that allegedly crashed at elk creek near Westport, Washington. The UFO we saw took a similar path from Elma towards Westport as the UFO that crashed in November of 1979.

The military showed up soon after that crash, sealed off the area and carted, whatever it was, off to who knows where? One witness said that another UFO matching the description of the first one showed up soon after the crashed one had been taken away by the military and seemed to look over the crash site. It then left southwest over the Pacific Ocean.

About six months later my cousins Joe, Amber and I saw one around mid-day. That sighting took place near Leavenworth Washington. We had hiked out from a backpacking trip into the cascades and were loading our gear back into the car. I spotted the object first at quite a distance and said something like "Look, there's a home built ultra-light coming." That was my first impression when spying the delta shaped object coming along the ridgeline above us. I could detect a pod of some sort below the main body of the craft and I interpreted that lump as the pilot. There was something odd about it though and I kept my eye on it. As it got closer, I drew the attention of my cousins to it again. It didn't look right. I then uttered something like "That doesn't look right?" After taking a look, my cousins were as puzzled as I was? As it got even closer, we started to say almost in unison, "What the F%@& Is That!" That was uttered several times among the three of us before the mysterious UFO had passed out of view. We were dumbfounded! There was a camera right there in the car about fifteen feet away and no one thought to pick it up.

The craft was silver, triangular shaped, between forty and one hundred twenty feet across. I'm taking into account how close a ridge line looks until you climb it, which made it hard to judge the size. It had no exhaust or propeller and no sound. It was drifting into a stiff wind coming from the southwest.

The reason I'm mentioning these UFO incidents is because I never saw one before I started to interact with the forest people. I've seen many others since. Three within the last few months leading up to this writing. Why do I see them so often now?

When Russell and I returned to the Becho location again, I decided not to scream anymore. Becho obviously didn't like it. I came to the understanding that it is an angry scream I was using. It's like going to someone's front door and screaming your head off expecting an invitation to enter. Besides, we were so close to where they lived it was unnecessary.

So, now what? I had no idea? We went back and started a fire, but decided not to camp. We could hear them approach very close from two sides. Becho had friends or family with him. I had brought a toy that makes a sort of UFO sound effect when I swing it around my head. I thought they might find it entertaining? After swinging it Russell told me he could hear them scramble away a little bit, as if it startled them. Oops. I put the toy away.

Around that time, Russell told me about one of his brothers witnessing rocks thrown into a pond while he was fishing. The pond is located about ten miles from the Becho landing. I went out to that pond, looked around and saw nothing other than a herd of elk. After getting back to the vehicle I stopped to pee and a branch broke very near and very loudly. It startled me a little and after trying to see what it was that broke the branch I, somewhat hastily, got into my car and left.

I had read somewhere that sasquatch like music, so I brought my guitar out to the Becho clan the next time. I played as Russell fell asleep in the camp chair. After I was done, I started to put the guitar back in its case when I heard, what sounded like a young girl go "Aww" in apparent disappointment at the ending of the show. She was right over my left shoulder and very close. There was a small berm there that she was hiding behind. I suddenly realized that the guitar was a hit! I woke up Russell and told him what had just happened. From then on, he would be the ears while I played.

We went out several times to hang out with them and play music for them. Russell could hear them faintly vocalize along and also some light tapping to some of the songs. He told me that their favorite song was my acoustic rendition of Echoes, by Pink Floyd. He based that judgement on their participation during the song. I decided they had good taste in music, since my favorite band of all time is Pink Floyd.

When I play for my forest friends, I try to mix it up. I might play folk, rock, blues, jazz, country and classical, all on the same night. I play a lot of originals for them as well. I even have a couple of sasquatch songs I wrote.

Between songs we could hear Becho's low voice talking to his sons. They always spoke in very hushed tones and were barely audible. Becho and his sons were always on one side and his mate and daughter were together on the other side. We could hear and distinguish each of their voices. That's how we knew they were a family of five with two sons, a mother, father and the youngest being a daughter. I tried to record their voices, but my equipment wasn't up to it. I needed a parabolic microphone set up. In fact, I still haven't gotten one.

It wasn't long and we felt quite at home with them. There is a calming effect that develops when they are around. It is a very deep and wonderous experience. I cherish every moment I've had with these great and mysterious beings. There is a certain ambience they generate that is hard to describe. I very much enjoy playing music for them. It feels like that is my special gift for them. I consider it a great honor. I've played for several other forest families since those early days with the Becho family.

One night I forgot to bring the camp chairs. I sat on the cooler and played while Russell paced back and forth around the landing. He was complaining of a sore leg when he tripped in the direction of one standing near the perimeter. When Russell saw him, he started to take off in one direction while I heard the sasquatch take off in the other. I heard the sasquatch run for about three steps before he realized no one was chasing him. He then moved around to where the mother and daughter were hiding behind the berm and settled back down. I got a little bit of a laugh from it. Russell's eyes were popping there for a moment as he began to run and then didn't. I believe it was the eldest son, based on Russell's description. He was about seven feet tall at that time.

I hadn't seen one yet, so I was a little disappointed that I was looking at Russell when it all came down. I missed my chance as the sasquatch was standing next to a young Hemlock where I could have easily spied him, if I had been looking that way. I believe he had maneuvered there to watch my fingering on the guitar as it was lit up by the fire. He was only about thirty feet away.

We also started to bring gifts. I set up a wooden bowl I had made on about a fourteen-inch-tall log round. I balanced it very precariously and then I'd put five or six apples in it. When we returned the apples would be missing and the round and bowl would still be upright. I knew no other animal was getting the apples. It had to be them. No other animal could pick out those six apples without tipping over the round. I could barely do it, myself.

I eventually went back to check out the pond where the rocks were thrown near Russell's brother. I hiked down to the pond and took a look around, but found nothing interesting other than a nice beaver dam. While hiking back up and after rounding a sharp corner I heard, what sounded like a coyote from where I had just been a few seconds before. I tried to see through the brush, but it was just thick enough to obscure whatever it was on the other side of that sharp bend? I was suspicious immediately upon hearing it, because I didn't think a coyote would do that? Coyote avoid humans like the plague and if it was a coyote, it certainly knew I was there and seemed to be howling to me. So, I howled back and got a return howl. After doing that a few times and getting a return call every time, I decided to create a pattern with my howling. I'd howl something like Woooo, woooo, woo, woo, woo, wooooo. Three times I changed the pattern of the howl and three times he imitated my howls perfectly. It made me laugh out loud. I'm sure he was highly amused, as well. I said, "Okay, that's enough, have a great day!" and hiked back to my car.

I was almost certain it wasn't Becho that played that howling game with me, even though it was only ten miles away and the direction Becho had come from when he screamed at us. I can't really say why I thought that, except to say I get very subtle feelings about them and usually they are correct. It seemed as though this other one knew about me and decided I was worthy of a practical joke? How did he know? We could hear them talk while we were at the Becho location. Did Becho give his friend or relative a description of me? Perhaps he told him that I was the one who wore a green hat and glasses? Maybe he was there when I played the guitar? It made me realize that they might be a lot more intelligent and sophisticated than I had imagined? The other revelation was that they have a sense of humor.

Around that time, I was told, by a friend about her encounters with sasquatch while working for the Fisheries. Connie has a few stories, but has never seen one.

Once, she was working on a creek with a partner. They split up and went different ways to count and take scale samples during a fish run. She returned first and was hiking up to the pickup truck when she heard something that froze her in her tracks. It was a whining deer in great distress. The sounds were coming from the creek where she had just been. She could also hear a lot of movement on the rocky gravel creek bed. Then she heard nothing, until she heard a very loud scream that chilled her to the bone. As she stood there frozen in place with paralyzing fear, she heard movement through the woods adjacent to the trail and then silence. She finally got her courage up to continue to the truck and lock herself in.

Her partner became way overdue, which worried her. He finally showed up walking down the access road they were parked on. He told her he was about to reach the trail leading up to the truck when he came upon the rear quarters of a deer. It had been torn in half and fresh blood was spattered on the surrounding trees. He was so freaked he retreated, found another way up to the road and then hiked back to the pickup truck. He told her that, just a few yards in front of the truck, was a blood line crossing the road.

After hearing the location, I decided that it was probably the Becho clan that had harvested the deer. Why just the front quarters of the deer? Organs are very nutritious, especially the liver. Perhaps, taking the organs back in the rib cage made for an efficient container?

She also told me of another location where she had some peculiar things happen? She was in a fish hole, full of fish when a limb came in and knocked her down. I believe they did not mean to hit her. The limb had bounced off of another limb of a tree she was under. She has also encountered demonstration charges by something she could not see, but hear. I went to that location soon after our conversation and saw a huge sasquatch on my first trip there.

I was hiking along a logging road and peering into the woods to the right. Then I began to turn my head to the left and a very dark, large sasquatch, who was only about fifteen feet from my right side, took off into the woods. I only saw him in my peripheral vision for a micro second. I snapped my head back to the right and he was already gone. I did see him well enough to interpret his size as extra, extra-large and tall. By the time I could get through the thick underbrush to take a better look, all was silent and appeared vacant.

As I walked by, he was blending into some spruce boughs. If I looked directly at him, I would have had a really good close look from less than fifteen feet away. When they stand still and are close to trees or brush, they are very effective at blending into the background.

Soon after, I went again to that same area. I had walked to the end of a spur where the brush was too thick to see through, but I could clearly hear some grumbling beyond. It was two sasquatch talking to each other. I didn't feel comfortable talking to them, so I stood there for a few moments and listened before I began to hike back out. As I passed another spur, I heard what sounded like a young girl scream from the end of it. I then knew it was the Becho clan that was there.

Now, I know that several families gather in that area for the salmon runs. I've found a lot of signs of juveniles playing in the trees there. Perhaps it is a place of reunion? I still go hiking on the many roads that spider web from that area and occasionally hear a knock. I do not know which sasquatch I saw there? I have a feeling it might be the one I now call teacher.

Eventually we started to take Russell's daughter, Kessa, out with us. She is an acute observer. Kessa has a sharp mind and is very good at coming up with a logical hypothesis. I promised her it would be less than a month before she would have her first experience. I believe it took around ten days.

Over several months of habituation, we made a few mistakes with the Becho clan including my building a smoky fire one night. The smoke wafted down the hill towards the Becho family and we started to hear whistles, bird calls and loud movement. The young daughter vocalized in distress with a sort of Ohhhh, ohhhhhh. She was upset because Becho was upset and it worried her. Becho and his two sons moved around and took up positions on two bluffs above our location. Becho to the west and his sons to the south. Then they called back and forth to each other. After the calls Becho pushed a tree down in disgust. You can check out the recording of this incident on You Tube, if you would like, with this link. Always use headphones. I use no audio filters on any of these throughout the book. https://youtu.be/WngirLnjatE

That happened to be the first night we brought Russell's daughter Kessa, with us to the Becho location. I had just bought an Olympus LS-20m video/audio recorder and had assigned its operation to her. She had turned it on just in time to record the calls and tree push down. It was also the first time I saw, what I thought, was the young girl peeking at us from around a tree that was across the raven. I think she heard Kessa talking and wanted to take a good look at her. It was still light enough for me to see her. As soon as I saw her, her head snapped back behind the tree.

Kessa is a brave young lady and didn't flinch from the calls or the sound of the tree being pushed down. But it was time to go. It was obvious Becho was upset and had enough of the smoky fire and every other misstep we had made along the way.

After a few days we went back near dusk and started to set up on a another landing a few hundred yards away and higher up the valley. I thought maybe they would be okay with us if we were further away.

It was a quiet, mild, early spring evening. We stood at the edge of the landing facing north. After we were there for about ten minutes, we started to hear Becho scream from the next valley to the north, which we could partially see from the edge of that landing. He would scream for about four seconds, then take a long breath and scream again. It was the angry scream. We could tell he was coming toward us. We recorded over fourteen minutes of his screams that night. The following is the link for that. I want to apologize for calling Russell an idiot on the recording. There were three of us buddies that used the term for each other in a carefree and loose manner back then, not really meaning it. https://youtu.be/xj99nrT2-84

I was pretty sure he was screaming at us. I wondered how he knew we were there? Had he seen us from a ridge on the other side of the valley? That ridge line looked like it was about five miles away. It was topped by a clear cut, so he would have had an unobstructed line of sight. Without binoculars I would have been hard pressed to see a vehicle over on that ridge. Did the son do some ultra sound thing to alert him to our presence? Did someone in the Becho family alert the patriarch via telepathy? I was a bit puzzled?

As we stood there listening, we could hear the eldest son come around below and circling around us from right to left. It was easy to track his progress, because of the frogs. Again, we knew exactly where he was at any given moment. He moved extremely fast over very difficult terrain. There is swamp and tree fall and all kinds of hazards to negotiate. He covered in ten minutes what would take me an hour and a half or more to traverse. When he arrived behind us, Kessa and I gave each other a knowing nod. There was an opening that led to an eroded gully on the other side of the vehicle, which he used to come up the hill. He was about ten yards past the vehicle and watching us from behind some thick brush at the top edge of that gully. I assumed it was the seven-foot-tall eldest son, who must have been left to watch over the family as Becho went, perhaps to hunt for food? We couldn't see him, but we knew exactly where he was.

As we stood there I came up with another theory, that it was Kessa's neon green jacket he could see from that far ridge? At the time, it was the same color the company that cleared the trees used on all of their vehicles and apparel. Kessa then took her coat off and he stopped screaming. Was it the jacket? By this time, I figured he could be on the tree line on the opposite ridge from us. Perhaps that is why he quit screaming?

I told Russell and Kessa that maybe they didn't like us anymore and perhaps we -should leave them alone. We packed up and left with a profound feeling of loss. We wouldn't go back there for fifteen months and only at Kessa's insistence. She wanted it for her high school graduation gift. How could I resist that?

The return was a special night. As soon as they realized it was us, we heard the young girl howl in delight. That made my heart soar. Then we heard a deep thump, as if a log had been lifted off the ground and then dropped. I took that as more of a recognition than a rejection. This is something I've heard on several occasions since.

We set up the camp-chairs, but we didn't start a fire. I broke out the guitar and we just sat there and talked and sang while twilight turned to dark. Just before it got too dark Kessa saw, what was probably the eldest son, parting some brush directly across from her. They all came and surrounded us and enjoyed the music. From that experience I learned that they were willing to forgive.

Within weeks of our happy reunion the logging company closed the gate to that area and we were locked out.

CHAPTER 3

Time to Expand

WE WERE ALL sad when we got locked out from the Becho clan. But since I had found the Becho clan, I reasoned that I could find others. Soon, I went out searching, armed with my list of parameters. I found another family very quickly and we started to visit them. Then I started to look farther and farther from home, eventually going all the way up into the Olympic mountains. In about six months I'd found six or more other families. It was a fun time. I'd pick a location and go there and make a call, then wait for something to happen. The locals would respond with a return call, knock, chest pounding, limb breaking, rock clacking or some other kind of noise. I'd move to another location and try again and it would work again.

I was amazed how successful I was and how common they were. For four years we struggled to find anything that I would call hard evidence of their existence. Now, it seemed, as if they were everywhere. I was even finding evidence, such as footprints, when I wasn't even looking for them. I also saw sasquatch, on occasion, during these adventures.

I found one family, almost living in the suburb of a small town. In that case I first found a fourteen-inch print (pictured below) while hiking a well-used trail. I didn't expect to find any evidence of a sasquatch there, because of the trail's proximity to a town. The forest person had been attempting to step across the trail, but at that point it was too wide and he came up a little shy. There was a flat hard surface with some dry pine needles. His foot was wet from off trail and the dry needles stuck to the bottom of his wet foot leaving a very nice impression. I looked for more prints off trail, but had no luck in that spongy, mossy undergrowth.

I then started to hike out there more often. One day I was looking at a cougar track when I looked up hill and saw a tall dark figure hiding behind a tight bunch of alder trees. He was almost completely obscured by the leaves and trunks of those trees. After I saw him, he quickly ducked behind the trees and disappeared. I figured he must still be there, because there didn't seem to be any place for him to hide while trying to slip away? I was pretty confident I would find him or see him, if he moved. I slowly walked up to that spot keeping my eyes on it at all times while attempting not to blink. By this time, I wasn't feeling any fear of them at all. I was looking forward to seeing this big guy up close. When I got up there, he was gone. I couldn't figure out how he could possibly have slinked away? There was a small, very shallow dip in the landscape that ran parallel to the ridgeline. But he seemed way too big to hide in it while he crawled away. His only option, without any trees or brush to hide behind, was to crawl. As I stood there looking around, my thought was "This is nuts!!! He should be right here!?"

I searched that ground very carefully for any sign of his crawling, but I saw none. There were no tracks anywhere. It was a spongy moss landscape and not very conducive to leaving tracks, but still, I thought I should have detected something? It seemed inexplicable that he could have gotten away from me without me seeing his exit?

When I began to hike back out, I felt him paralleling me from across the small river. In places there isn't a lot of undergrowth under the mature trees, so I was listening and watching for him. I knew he was there, even though I couldn't hear or see him. I stopped to look at an alder that had been broken off and balanced almost straight up and down, leaning against a very weak branch of another alder. I could see the stump where the tree had been broken off from and it didn't seem possible that the wind blew it into that position. It would have had to do all kinds of maneuvers to get there without breaking some limbs of the tree it was leaning against.

As I was filming that tree, he snuck up behind me along the river embankment and shook the brush. He was very close. I'd say less than ten yards away, yet I couldn't see him or maneuver where I could see him. He had picked the perfect spot. I never considered him dangerous so I just filmed in his direction and talked to him. In the video you can hear one crack of a twig from behind the thick brush. Some have told me that they can see him in the video, but I've never been able to make him out. You can check and see if you can spot him on YouTube with the following link. https://youtu.be/3TLy5yujCak

I chose the location where I was standing when I saw him for leaving gifts of energy bars and nuts when I went out there. I noticed an ex made from two good size hemlocks the next time out. I thought it might have been them that did it?

It is commonly believed, by many of the bigfooting community, that an ex means friendship or family. I leave them ex's too. Mine are just a couple of crossed branches.

Recently I found a beautiful sculpture in that area made by breaking branches and then wrapping them around a tree trunk. The branches then healed in position and became covered in deep green moss. It's very unusual looking and gorgeous!

One day I was putting gifts on a log for them when I turned and saw, what I believe was a young forest girl. She was only visible for a moment. I saw her arm and shoulder as she ducked behind a young hemlock about a hundred yards away. She was about five and a half feet tall and her hair was light brown with blond high lights. The only blondie I've seen so far. I had heard something in the brush while hiking out and had the thought that it might be a youngster hiding in there. I even got the impression, for some reason, that it was a she. I looked at the brush when I heard her, but I didn't look in. I had the impression of a juvenile being in there as I walked past.

As I hiked back past where I originally heard her in the brush, I spied an upside-down mushroom on a log. That mushroom was the first gift I ever received from one of them. I took a picture of it, but I didn't touch it, because I figured they might be able to metabolize foods that would kill us. I wasn't sure if it was a mushroom or a toadstool? I think she might have been hurt by my rejection of her gift. She picked the mushroom up and transferred it to another part of the trail, but I had taken a detour and missed seeing it until I went hiking out there a couple of days later. It was mush by then, the room had left.

I eventually made the mistake of leaving my recorder on and forgetting it on the gifting stump. It only took me about five minutes to realize what I had done. So, I returned to the log and picked it up, stopped the recorder and deleted the recording without checking it. I didn't think they had been there yet, but I was mistaken. After about ten minutes of hiking back out I began to hear screaming coming from the distance. I turned on my recorder and got about seven minutes of those angry vocals. Then an airplane flew over and he was done. It took a few days for it to dawn on me that he was screaming because he saw the recorder on the log. Oops. Here is the link to his screams on You Tube. https://youtu.be/m_zHvV_t8QA

On a camping trip to the Olympics, I was the only person in the campground when I heard a metallic sound emanating from the far end of the campground. When I went to investigate, I found two small saplings that were crossed on a trail adjacent to the campground. I took out my camera and started to record. While I was filming, I heard a light wood knock from behind me. In the video my shadow is in the frame and you can see my head snap around in the direction of the knock. It wasn't until I got home that I realized the metallic sound could have been someone checking the campground's bear proof food storage unit? When I returned the next time, I tested that hypothesis by opening and closing the locker and sure enough the sound was the same.

Again, I got the immediate impression that they were female juveniles, even though I hadn't seen or heard any of their vocals yet. My hunch would be proven correct later. How did I know?

About three weeks later Russell Wilson, Kessa and I hiked out to where I believed the young females lived. This was just over a mile from the campground. Kessa found juvenile prints right on the trail. One set was a little bigger than my foot and the other quite a bit smaller. Something I've noticed is that they spread the age out between children. They seem to be about three or four years apart.

We also heard them while we were out there, including whoops and what sounded like a chest pounding. On the hike back out I had a very strong feeling that we were being shadowed. Kessa stopped to play on a very large Douglass fir log that was balanced across another downed log, creating a natural teeter totter. She was having fun tipping it back and forth while jumping on it. I was keeping my eye on the ridge. I was thinking they would like Kessa's playfulness and if they were there, they'd be watching. I saw nothing, but felt they were there.

We ate lunch at the campsite where I camped the time before and kessa saw one of the girls. Kessa was seated across from her dad and I at a picnic table. Behind Russell and I and across the camp access road, was thick foliage. There was some shorter, four-foot-high brush, creating a break among the higher flora. She said she saw a flash of dark brown hair flash by in that small gap. I dismissed it at first as, perhaps a bird? Then a couple of minutes later we all heard the mother call. The two juvenile females screamed back to their mother while they were very close to us. They had moved to the other side of us and onto the main road. They sounded like two pre-teen human girls screaming at a concert. They were obscured by thick brush and trees and less than fifty yards away. They were outside their play territory was my thinking at the time. There was an isolated creek over where the mother had screamed from. My thought was the mother had walked the length of their play territory looking for her daughters and when she didn't find them, she screamed for them. I then knew Kessa had seen one and apologized for doubting her.

I went back soon after and took Tanya German, a film maker friend of mine. I didn't want her to bring a camera just in case they might not like it? I did bring casting material and we made a cast of one of the prints. Tanya did hear a low whoop or two from the girls during the visit. While we were waiting for the cast to dry, hikers would pass by and one actually said, "Bigfoot!?" I reluctantly replied in the affirmative and he and his wife hiked up the trail only to return, hiking back out, after just a couple of minutes. I believe they decided the creep factor might have been too great? I could hear the girls about thirty yards away, obscured by thick brush and talking in hushed tones. I told Tanya they were there, but I don't think she could hear them? Then I heard, what I thought at first, was a foreign speaking hiker coming up the trail. Soon, I realized it was the mother who had come for the daughters. She was talking to her daughters for a few moments and then they all left. I would love to know what she was telling them? Again, Tanya couldn't hear what I was hearing. I was a bit closer to them than she was.

I have only been back there a few times since. I did go for a couple of day visits in 2019 and Russell and I heard two males and a female call from different directions. That brings up an interesting point. When Russell and I were hiking that day there was an Asian family that we had passed just before we heard the first call. The call came from over the small hill we were at the base of and very clear. Yet, when I retreated a few feet and asked the Asian family if they had just heard the sasquatch, they all replied "No!". They obviously weren't paying attention to the surrounding sounds of the forest. That first call was clear as day and did not sound like a bird. City folk?

Kessa, Russell and I also went on a one-night camping trip at a location where I had an encounter with another forest person. I was driving around the Olympic foot hills when I spied a suspicious broken tree. I spent a lot of time meandering around that area and found, what I believe, was a rodent trap. It was built out of flat rocks and located next to the access road. It was placed where it caught the sun all day in the winter. It had one slot to crawl into. I figured the idea was that a critter would crawl into the shelter to get warm and then he would come and harvest it. Since then, I've found other piles of rocks, in that general area, that I believe were assembled for the same purpose.

As I was getting ready to leave, I began to relieve myself near my Subaru. I heard what sounded like something sliding down an embankment in the woods across from where I was doing my business. Then I heard a series of knocks as if whoever, was moving away and hitting each tree with a limb as he passed. That was almost comical and confirmed my suspicions that there was a sasquatch hanging out there. He was watching me and knew what I was looking for. Especially since I was admiring his engineered rodent trap so much. So, why did he move and begin to knock? To let me know I was right about my suspicions? It seemed he wanted me to know he was there.

Later, when Russell, Kessa and I went for an overnight camping trip there, Russell saw that forest person. He was white and I have come to realize that he's also a loner, perhaps an elder?

By this time, we had gotten a reputation around town for what we were doing. Russell got a call one evening from one of his brothers and a neighbor of his brother telling him that they could hear what they thought might be bigfoot, calling up in the foothills adjacent to their homes. Russell and I hiked up there and I made a call. It was my pathetic attempt at their angry roar, as I've come to understand. A couple of minutes after my call there was a return roar that wasn't so pathetic. I looked at Russell and said, "Yep, they're up here." and we walked back out. We still have a good laugh at how casual we were about the whole thing after all we had experienced over the prior few years.

That particular family I visit on occasion and they interact in subtle ways as most of the locals around my home town do. I might hear a vocal, branch break or a wood knock. I've even heard them from my home.

In 2019 I hiked into a local area and upon my hike out I found a freshly built sculpture in my path, that wasn't there on the way in. It consisted of two rocks the size of softballs, with a golf ball size rock perched on top and a smaller rock at the base. I believe it could have been a representation of their family. This family is a mystery to me at this writing and this is one of the only clues I have of them.

At the same time people were hearing them on the south side of the valley, I talked to some friends who live on the north side of the valley and they were hearing them too. They went on making vocals off and on for a few days, or weeks and then it was over. It's hard to say why they suddenly decided to be heard by the townspeople? I'm sure they were aware they could be heard.

I talked to a friend who lives up on a ridge above the south fork area and he said he's heard them many times. I also talked to a young lady one day that lives in the same area as my friend and she said the bigfoot howls creep her out. I told her not to worry about them, the calls are not about her.

We also found another forest family about a half hour drive from my home in Raymond Washington. That is a beautiful spot, overlooking a steep cut canyon. When I stand at the top of a gorgeous valley like that, I feel a deep connection to nature. That valley has been there for a long time and so have they. Kessa, Russell, Alex, Neil and I had some nice nights there. We might turn a bright lantern on and cover it with a white towel, or just stare at the stars with the lights turned out. One night I was gazing up when I saw a huge meteor that lit up the sky for about four seconds. Out there the night sky is stellar.

We kind of knew the routine by then, as far as introductions. On the first night it was Russell, Kessa and I. I stood at the edge of the landing and talked to the forest people, who I assumed lived across the valley in the direction of my speaking. I Told them that we would like to be friends. We could hear them talking to each other near the location I thought they would be. Then on the adjacent landing a tree was pushed over. We didn't take the tree push down that seriously. I felt it was a display by the patriarch of his concern for his family and a show of strength. He was letting us know that it was his valley. We all knew he was the king of that valley without question. We were also very determined not to be turned away.

We settled in and played music while relaxing, joking and enjoying our night. I brought my amp and one of my Stratocasters and hooked up to my car battery, so that they could hear it from anywhere in the valley. We could hear some movement on the wider perimeter. There was twig cracking behind a slash pile that was only about thirty yards away and another one moving on the opposite side, up a wildlife trail.

The next time we went out there we repeated everything. I stood on the edge of the landing and gave a nice speech, then we heard some talking and then we heard another tree go down. It was déjà vu, all over again.

That landing soon got blocked off by a logging company, but the one where we heard the trees go down was still open, so we moved to that location. After we played music the first night, Russell and I returned during the day and we found the two trees that were pushed down. They were two alder trees, side by side and about the same size at five or six inches thick. The breaks were about six or seven feet off the ground.

As we approached the alders, we both felt a chill. Then we heard a branch break, quite close, from around the corner of the log road we were on. I felt like they didn't want us to go any further and that was fine with me. We got to hear, a few times, the elder son and daughter talking while hiding behind some thick brush and young trees. I loved hearing them talk during the day. We knew exactly where they were and they knew we would respect their space and not try to go looking for them. I did try and steal a peek through the brush as we walked by where they were hiding, but I never managed to see them.

I started taking my friends Alex and Neil out there. We went out during the day once and took a tour of the area. Alex spotted a limb hanging down in a peculiar manner. I noticed there were four limbs overlapping like ropes hung the length of the tree, top to bottom. I had the thought that they might have done that to make climbing easier for a very little juvenile. I went back after the leaves fell to get some unobstructed video of it when I noticed that the tops of many alders were bent over. I've only seen this in a few places since and never as common as they were in that area. There was a junction of log road spurs, surrounded by alder trees, that served as their playground. It was like the juveniles were using it as a huge jungle gym and romper room. All the tops of the trees surrounding that junction had limbs bent over. Here is the Facebook link to my analysis, https://youtu.be/-I5RC-d101Y

People often ask how we can tell who is who? It's because we hear them. The boys sound like boys and the girls sound like girls. The women and men sound like women and men. Except some of those males have very deep voices. Just like you can recognize human voices, we recognize individual sasquatch by their voices and habits.

They came to accept our friendship and we created a gifting area for them. We'd set up and play music for them and like the Becho family, they would come and listen. After my friends Alex and Neil played a very beautiful song one night, we heard a young infant scream in delight from not so far away. That thrilled us so much! So, my hunch that they pulled those branches down for a small one might have been correct?

Russell came with me during the day soon after we heard the young one that night. After we arrived at the landing I whooped and got a return whoop from the young juvenile male. We heard the infant scream twice more during that visit.

Russell suggested we leave a teddy bear for the infant. Our next trip out, Russell brought a very small teddy bear and put it in a tree. It lingered there for a few weeks before I took it and placed it behind the gifting stump. We could hear the boy and girl whispering to each other, so I talked to them and told them, while holding up the teddy bear, that it was a gift for them. I got so excited when I returned to check and the teddy bear was gone.

While driving back down to town after finding out they accepted the teddy bear, I saw the patriarch. He was standing where I could see him for only a couple of seconds while driving past. It was a place I always look when I drive by, because it is one of the few places the creek bed is visible along that stretch of road. I am sure he knew that I always look through that tunnel of foliage. On that day the view was almost completely blocked by a huge silhouette. The silhouette looked like a large tree stump with a knot on top of it. I knew that view, very well and quickly realized that I'd never seen a stump in that gap before. He was only in view for about two seconds, but that was enough. He had given me the gift of a visual and I was so happy! That family became known as the teddy bear clan.

I have been asked a few times why I didn't hit the brakes and back up? He would have been gone by then. He chose that location to give me a two second visual and that is all I was being allowed. I knew that.

Soon after, that area with the junction playground was put off limits by a logging company. I've returned up there a few times, but the situation of so much closed area makes it impossible to return for an evening of music. We would have to park on the side of the main access road and that would not work. People actually drive that road to commute between small communities.

Since we were locked out, I believe I've heard three stories about the Teddy Bear clan. All of them took place before we befriended them and very close to where they live.

One story was about a camping trip by two or three men. They pushed a log off a landing to get it out of the way. Then, after setting up their tent and other parts of the camp, the log came flying back up the hill, smashing the tent. They quickly scrambled into their rig, stuck it in gear and left everything right where it was, never to return.

Another witness told me he was berry picking in that area and somehow ended up very close to a mother and two children eating berries within feet of him. He was in awe at first and then he started to interact with the young ones. He and the children had fun smearing their faces with berries and making faces at each other. The mother tolerated the antics for a few minutes before finally herding the kids away. Then I was told of a hunter who saw a whole family sitting on a log in that valley.

A lady I know had an incident in that valley around 1970. She was with friends and then separated to go relieve herself in the woods. As she was stooped down, she felt a presence and looked up to see a huge sasquatch standing a few feet away, watching her. It scared the piss out of her! I knew this lady for years before she found out I was interacting with sasquatch and told me her story. That is the way it is in a small town.

I've heard a few stories that I'm sure were generated by encounters with the Becho clan. Those stories I hadn't known about before we began interaction. It's interesting to read eye witness accounts now about forest people I know. At the Quinault Sasquatch Summit in Ocean Shores a presenter showed a picture of two track lines in the snow up in the Wynootchee area. I'm sure those tracks were made by friends of mine. I also read an account about a hiker who was banging on trees to let the bear know he was there. That annoyed, probably those same friends of mine, even though it was in another valley. He was chased all the way back out to the parking lot with a shove in the back for good measure.

I read a story in BFRO of a guy who had an encounter with the eldest son of the Becho family while hunting. He had dropped off his daughter and boyfriend and then drove down to the same landing where we had interactions and came upon a young, big teen on a stump. They stared into each other's eyes for a few moments, in fear. The hunter said they were both scared to death! He whipped the pick-up around and drove out, picked up his daughter and her boyfriend and skedaddled.

That large stump is still there. Russell Wilson eventually met this man and says he told him he will never go back there. Sasquatch are everywhere there is a patch of wilderness, so not going back to that area strikes me as an unnecessary exercise.

Another man that was hunting in the same area came upon a huge sasquatch. He said they gazed at each other for a brief time, the sasquatch said something in a language he didn't understand, then disappeared into the thick woods.

We have also found them by going to locations of testimonials I've read. By the year 2014, it became just me. My friends Alex and Neil moved to Florida, Russell had moved away and Kessa was in college.

In the spring of 2014, I started camping up in the southern Olympics, near another forest family I had found. This family and their cousins have become very important and close to me. I had whooped and clacked rocks the first time I went there and heard a chest beating in reply. Later that night I had to get out of my tent to relieve myself and what sounded like a ten-year-old boy screamed at me from the woods. That juvenile I now call Peter. Peter does not sound like a ten-year-old boy anymore.

The next trip up there I hiked through the woods and heard tree knocks along the way, as if they were signaling to each other where I was and what direction I was going. I thought it fun and even reversed course after hearing a knock one time in an attempt to throw them off.

You might be wondering how many times they've been around my tent at night? The answer is, many, many times. One night, that same summer, I heard Jacque walk up from behind and then around to the front of my tent. I wondered what he would do if I unzipped the door? So, I unzipped and he just stood there about ten feet away. Then I wondered what he would do if I stuck my head out and tried to look at him? I stuck my head out only to find that it was pitch black and I couldn't see a thing. Jacque thought I could see him though and took off running down the trail. There was a cluster of trees where I heard him stop and probably hide behind? That was fun, but I was disappointed that I couldn't see him. There was a moon out that night, but I had camped under a thick canopy of trees. To this day I still haven't seen any of my forest friends up in the Olympics in the flesh, even though I've had a lot of interaction with them.

One-time Jacque bent a branch down and scraped it on the top of my tent to wake me up. I was already awake. His mom called and he left right away. That is always my experience when any youth have been near and then called back home by either parent. The young seem to be very obedient to their parents.

The next summer I returned armed with a 24-hour Sony recorder I could set out overnight. The first time I put it out Jacque came and woke me up. Then he went off through the woods for several yards and made a weird call. After he called, I heard a knock in the distance. Later upon review of the recording I realized that while Jacque was waking me up, he had detected the recorder and tapped the mic. I had hidden it under a flap on the tent, yet he knew it was there? I found that puzzling?

After posting the sound on the internet I got a lot of negative comments about it just being an owl. I knew better, even though it was the first time I'd heard such a vocal. Jacque had moved in the direction from which the vocal came. Why did he go if it wasn't to make the vocal without blaring it in my ear? Also, the knock, right after the vocal, appeared to be made in response and probably was his brother Peter. Another link to You Tube. https://youtu.be/cBfT6ZDkkHM

If I were to explain how I know, I would put it in terms of tracking. Not long ago, I went for a hike and found two elk herds. One of them I found because of the very fresh and voluminous scat connected with tracks that led off of a spur into some thick, young trees. I couldn't see them, hear them or smell them, but I knew about where they were, lying low until the hunters leave and the moon comes out. None of the hunters were aware of them, because they hadn't checked out that short spur road. The other herd I found had crossed the main log road and left one pile of fresh scat along the way. I could smell them and knew they were very close, hidden in some young trees. Just before I passed that spot, a hunter passed and was apparently clueless to the herds location. That herd had been hanging around there for days. I smelled them three times in almost the same place over the course of several days. Several hunters had passed that location over that period of time and apparently had their noses turned off.

These are things I've learned by going out to the wilderness thousands of days and hundreds of nights over a period of several years. I always look for tracks and try to read them. I've learned a thing or two along the way.

For instance, what an elk herd smells like. I don't consider myself a great tracker. I've read books about great trackers and I'm not even close to being in their league. I do know what I have learned and how to use all of my senses. I've learned the hunter's habits and the elk's habits. It is interesting to go hiking during the hunting season and watch the dance between the two sides. The humans, by the way, are a bit easier to predict, which is what the herds do. I've noticed most hunters really are clueless. When I used to hunt, I was clueless too. It takes time to learn out there.

I usually know where the herds are hiding and I keep it to myself. I believe I killed a bull before, because I talked too much one time. Right after that incident I herded some elk to safety just before the hunters got there, to make up for my loose lips. A few local elk herds know me and don't see me as a threat. So, it wasn't easy to convince them to move. I almost had to walk up and slap one on the rear to get them go. I herded them across a swollen creek where I knew the hunters wouldn't go. Other than that, one time, I leave both sides to their own devices and fate.

People need to understand that those wild animals are much more aware than most would believe. One day, during hunting season, I hiked right behind a herd. They were less than fifty yards away and the whole herds attention was uphill. They had their rears to me as I approached. They turned and looked down at me and then looked back up hill. They knew there were hunters up that hill and that was their focus. They also knew I wasn't a threat. I've even had them walk towards me when I've talked gently to them. It may be a generational memory for them? In that same general area, my dad had been in a school bus sometime in the thirties, when they stopped to feed the elk cigars by hand. It was against the law to shoot them back then and the herds were enormous and tame.

I and my friends have learned to interpret sasquatch without seeing them. Interpreting what you hear and smell can be even more telling than what you see. At one point, Russell, Kessa and I compared notes with each other on the Becho family. How many in the family? What is the mix between male and female? What are the ages of the children? Our impressions were consistent with each other's.

Everywhere I go camping now I hear "owls", almost every night. I've heard them in California, Oregon and Washington. If they are owls then why didn't I hear them that frequently before the idea of bigfoot was in my consciousness? I always know when it's Jacque, Peter and C.C. They have a trio style all their own.

Jacque and his cousins move around a greater territory in the southern Olympics. There are three families that are very close and move in unison. They have about 250 to 350 square miles of territory between the three families. They move back and forth among the valleys within that territory. Within each valley they spread the three families out to give each other a little space. So, when I first go looking for them and can't find them at one location, I just move over to the next valley and try again. Eventually, I will find where they will be hanging out for a few months.

It's always so fun when I hear them call to me for the first time of the season. I can tell that they are excited when they come to greet me. It is a great feeling to know that they care. I'm excited as well. I miss them when it's been a while.

One day I went hiking in their territory and passed some young alders that were all leaved out. I thought I heard a deep voice as I passed those young trees. I stopped and looked behind me and then dismissed it as my imagination and continued on my hike. Three hours later I came back past the same spot and heard that voice again. This time I was right next to it, so I knew I had heard right. He spoke in a language I couldn't understand, in a very deep voice. I faced the alders and stated that I wasn't trying to harm them in any way or bother them. I was just curious and thought "We might become friends?" I tapped my heart as I said it. I waited for a reply, but none came.

The next day I went behind those alders looking for tracks. I found no tracks, but there was a sculpture made of small sand stone rocks. At the time I thought it had been Jacque, but now I believe it was C.C. who spoke to me. C.C. used to stand for Crazy Cousin, not because I think he's crazy, but because he is very bold in the things he does. Recently I changed the meaning of C.C. to Cedar Crow. It just seems more respectable and I have a great amount of respect and love for all my forest friends. C.C. often mimics a crow like sound while the others are sounding like owls, thus the name. I left that sculpture there that day and then, about a week later, went back to collect it. It was gone. I regret now that I didn't take it and re-assemble it in my home. To me it looks like a self-portrait of him kneeling behind the foliage. This link is a video on

Facebook that describes my incident while showing wood sculptures that were nearby. https://youtu.be/AQbNtzlIJfk

I also found some, shelter like, structures during my wonderings around there. Russell Wilson wanted to see them, so I took him out there. We had to hike a short distance and at one point a helicopter came roaring over. It was dark green with insignia or markings too small to discern. It flew around making sharp turns and then, at one point, came down and hovered over the river bed to view us. Then it left.

As soon as it got out of ear shot, Jacque or his father roared from not far away. Then another sasquatch roared from up the valley. Then C.C.'s father roared. This was about noon and we got a big laugh out it. They did not like that helicopter one bit! That was their way of flipping it off.

In early April of 2016 I went up to the Olympics for my first camping trip of the season. It was an unusually hot day for that time of year. I set up camp in a popular no fee area, because I thought I'd be alone that early in the season on a weekday. The place I was originally going to camp was blocked off with a freshly built dirt obstacle.

Much to my surprise, three young ladies showed up and camped about a hundred yards away and another single man camped about fifty yards beyond them. I could see the young ladies camp from my camp, so, I really didn't expect anything to happen that night. Especially since I had camped, in what I presumed at the time, to be outside Jacque and his family's territory. I was aware that there was another forest family close to where I set up camp, but I really didn't think they knew me? I had heard them vocalize a couple of times from where I presumed, they lived. That was way up the mountain on a steep incline from where I was camping.

I did have hints that something might be up, soon after I got there I went on a hike. I crossed a foot bridge made out of a log, which I took a few minutes to admire. Upon my return to that foot bridge, just a few minutes later, there was a small tree that had fallen across the creek in the interim and some of the branches were lying across the bridge. I thought it was likely the tree didn't fall on its own, so I checked the base of the tree for prints or any other sign and didn't see any? This wasn't far from where I heard the voice emanate from behind the young alders that one day. At this writing I've come to the conclusion that it was C.C. who fell the tree and talked to me from behind the young alders. He also rustled some brush once while I was on that trail.

As I stood there near the creek bed and footbridge, I was surrounded by a horseshoe ridgeline about forty feet up and two thirds around in circumference. I took a look at every inch of the ridge line, but didn't see anyone. Now, I know C.C. was somewhere up there laughing at me under his breath. As the joke goes, they are world champs at hide and seek. I gave up and started to hike out again.

I believe one of the things they like about me is that I'm not knocking or vocalizing in their faces since those very early days. I also don't attempt to chase them or find them anymore. It's been a process of learning. I did come to the conclusion that it was unnecessary to make any calls, or knocks. I hardly ever initiate vocals anymore. I do sometimes return a call or a knock once in a while, when I'm sure there are no humans around. Or, when I figure the humans around are clueless. But, generally speaking, I leave all the knocking and vocalization for them to do. I also don't push any trees down. I figured there was a very good chance that a juvenile was up there somewhere smirking at me. I played it cool and left the interaction up to him.

Speaking of pushing trees down, there are many different reasons for them to push them down. They might be mad, or just saying hello, or attempting to guide me, or for marking something? It is for us to attempt to interpret in each individual case what the reason is? One time, while out in the Olympics, I mentioned tree push downs in passing to my friend Curt Harris and his granddaughter Indigo. I had the thought how cool it would be to hear one. It wasn't long and we heard one go down way up on a ridge above us. At that time, I wondered if Jacque had actually heard me mention tree push downs and then scrambled up to that ridge? Or, if he heard me telepathically? I was puzzled?

They had built huge structures or sculptures as I consider them, in this forest in the Wynootchee area. They used mature trees broken off and crisscrossed this way and that. The stumps of those trees could not be located by me. Then they would pull a vine maple over the top which framed the artwork. Once, near there, I found a noble fir log leaning up against a hemlock, in a hemlock grove. There was no sign of a stump or noble fir close by. It was placed right at a ninety degree turn of the trail, so, it would be directly in line of sight as the hiker walked towards it from either direction. Was I the only one that noticed? I looked at it the first time I passed, but didn't understand why it struck me as unusual, until I returned and saw it again.

Eventually that section of Federal Forest was marked for logging. My forest friends dismantled their artwork and disappeared the logs. There was no way any equipment was brought in for that. If equipment had been used, it would have scarred up the woods. It had to be my forest friends.

Also, a log had been pushed over onto an access road that was on one boundary of that survey. Several logs had been pushed down across the trail near the trail head, as well. It was obvious to me that they had been very upset over these developments. They understand perfectly, the various color codes the surveyors use and every phase of the logging operation.

The above is commonly called and asterisk.

My hike back out was uneventful, yet full of suspicion? It is amazing how quietly they can shadow someone without a sound. I kind of felt he was there and yet was unable to detect him.

I usually don't start a fire, but that night the wind was light and blowing away from where I knew it could bother any forest family. I started a small, hot fire, that I could enjoy as it turned from dusk to dark. I did my usual and played my guitar until I got tired and turned in. I was close enough to hear the ladies applaud after one song. I heard something on the other side of the brush when I relieved myself before retiring to my tent. A little rustle of the brush that made me smile at the thought that they might be there enjoying the music. My reasoning is that no wild animal would sneak up on my campsite to listen to music? Therefore, it is likely it was one of my forest friends. I've experienced something similar to this a few times.

I could hear the ladies laughing and settling in for the night. It was an unusually warm night and the moon was full. It was a perfect night, with still winds and mild temperatures. I had my window flap open and I could see the trees glowing blue from the moonlight.

Not long after I crawled into my sleeping bag, I began to hear a juvenile male, a few hundred yards away, chanting on top of a ridge directly above. I really have a hard time describing the chant. It was a blend of four different stylized animal sounds. In other words, not a direct mimic of any animal. The four sounded like a grouse, cat, elk and crow, maybe? He was very loud!

I smiled at myself knowing that the other campers must be hearing what I'm hearing and wondering what they might be thinking? Could they possibly have an idea of what it was they were hearing?

Suddenly, I realized that he was coming off of the ridge and making a beeline towards my campsite. The unexpected development startled me a little. That rush of adrenaline quickly faded away as I started to search, frantically, for my recording device. I had so much stuff in my tent that I couldn't find it. Meanwhile, he was coming so fast that I soon gave up on the idea of recording the event. I didn't want to be searching through my gear while he was in my encampment, so I stopped looking and laid back for the whatever it was going to be?

Soon he was in my campsite chanting very loud and moving in rhythm to his chant. A literal sasquatch chant and dance. I could tell by listening where he moved as he danced around. The first thing he did was move to a point where he could check and make sure the ladies were still in their tents. Then he moved around to the other side of my car to take a peek and see if my tent window was open? The whole time I'm staring out the window of the tent at the blue trees, just in case he came in front of it. He then retreated around the back of my vehicle and came right at the tent. I didn't sit up and peek because I always give them all of the power. I was hopeful that he would pass in front of my window and give me a visual, but alas, he went behind my tent instead. I was busy looking out the window and didn't even see his shadow, which was probably visible on the back-tent wall. I had the tent sucked up, rather close, against a couple of trees. He had to have almost touched my tent when he went by.

After his departure, he kept his chant going all the way back up to the ridge, only faltering a little towards the end. In other words, he was fast, strong and displayed a level of fitness that was beyond anything I had ever witnessed. It was a great gift and to this day I thank C.C. for being a bit different and more outlandish than the others. That is what makes him special. Every time I think of C.C. I get a big smile on my face.

Later, about one o'clock in the morning, I heard Jacque or his father. His call woke me up. He was about a half mile away across Wynootchee lake and made a beautiful, celebratory vocal. Then I heard two more, from different areas, repeat his vocal. It was very humbling to listen to that. I knew then, as I know now, they were all giving me a "hello". I could tell how happy they were. I was happy too. About four O'clock in the morning they repeated their vocals and then a few minutes later I heard the old white-haired loner from way up the valley. In one night, I had heard the forest friends from three families and the loner, plus was gifted an amazing visitation. It is one of my favorite nights of all time.

I walked down to the ladies the next morning and asked if they had heard anything the night before? "Yes!!! What was that!!!? A bear!!!?" No, it was not a bear and I informed them what it really was and what happened the night before. After telling them, their mouths were dropped and they stared at me with stunned silence. So, I said "Have a nice day." and began to walk back to my rig. They returned the kindness as I walked.

I then drove up to the plateau beyond that ridge and took a look around. That is the day I found the dome. Here is a video of that day and another when I took my friend Curt Harris a few days later. https://youtu.be/8Y62A2qilpQ

CHAPTER 4

The Playhouse

Now is when it starts to get weird folks, so fasten your seat belts. Okay, some of you might be laughing at that declaration after what you've just read, but I mean it.

I've always wanted to keep an open mind about everything. However, if there was a rational explanation for a seemingly anomalous event, I would make an effort to lean that way. I've always tried to stray away from magical thinking over strange events. I'm not inclined to believe in conspiracy theories either. Though, I will admit a couple of them make me go "Mmmmm?". That Mmmmm, would be strictly based on careful consideration of empirical evidence. I also believe everything has a scientific explanation and I want to know what that explanation is? I'm very curious!

Album cover for my musical, Haunted Hannan Playhouse. Skellring is my band name.

In the nineteen eighties, I heard someone clear their throat right behind me while I was standing next to the Hannan playhouse stage. I turned and looked and there was no one there. At the time, Dave Lund was in the house and I yelled to him to find out where he was? He was way back in the wood room at the back of the building and I could barely hear his reply. I quickly rushed outside the building and there was no one to be seen. The playhouse is on the quiet side of town across from a large city park that was, at the time, deserted. I dismissed it as maybe a glitch in my brain, perhaps? Sure, there were plenty of ghost stories about that old playhouse, but I wasn't going to assume that I heard a ghost, or spirit. I felt like I had a very open mind, but I always utilized metacognition to check my beliefs, as much as I can. I logged it into the mystery catalogue of my brain and didn't take it too seriously.

Over the decades I've heard many strange tales about ghostly occurrences at the Hannan Playhouse. I was intrigued, but not convinced. One of the most interesting stories was about a black cat. That story is from the seventies. At this time the stage had walls very close off stage right and left. A witness told me that during a rehearsal back in the 70s, the whole cast saw a black cat enter from the stage left wall, walk across the stage and exit out the stage right wall. The whole cast was stunned!

About ten years ago I was cleaning the audience seating at the playhouse, folding up each chair after my cleaning. That way I could keep track of the ones I'd already cleaned. There was a costume draped on the last chair in the first row, so I took it to the lobby. When I returned, two of the chair seats I put up were back down. Again, I dismissed it as my forgetful, glitchy brain. When I tested the chairs one of them was actually not that easy to drop back down. It sticks in the up position a little bit. I decided that either I made a mistake, or there really are ghosts? I chose the former. Why?

We are trained very well and thoroughly at a young age to dismiss such thoughts. There must always be a rational explanation for everything. What I mean by rational, is an explanation that is based on modern cultural sensibilities.

It astounds me that so many of us still manage to deny such considerations? How is it that we dismiss every witness and every piece of evidence so easily when it comes to the strange, cryptic or the metaphysical? Are we afraid? I did not feel frightened at the prospect of a ghost, I just felt there was probably another explanation? Perhaps the fear wasn't of the ghost, but of the ostracism? This is something I hear frequently when I talk to witnesses. They don't share because they would be laughed at, or worse?

We all want to belong. I certainly I am no exception. When you are a part of a tribe or culture you want to fit in. So, you adapt to their belief system. We are all indoctrinated into our perspective cultures from a young age, before we even think to question. A culture has a denial system that is adhered to through persuasion, peer pressure, threat of persecution, or indoctrination. I was adhering to it because I didn't know any better and the fear of being ostracized. I unconsciously went into default mode and didn't consider ghosts or spirits because it was less complicated not to. I was caught up in the system of denial.

Finally, after three decades, in the fall of 2017, I would see the ghost who cleared his throat behind me. At least, I think it was him. The night before the sighting, I had detected the ghost standing behind me as I was seated and directing a youth play. I was about three rows from the back corner and once in a while I could hear the folding chairs, that were leaned up against the wall, move a little. I could also sense his presence. I actually turned and smiled at him at one point, even though I couldn't see him. I was trying to let him know "It's okay that you are there, just don't cause any trouble."

The next night he was there again, but I forgot about him and after giving notes I charged back towards my seat. My sudden move spooked him, pun intended and he ran down the middle isle, went up on stage and touched one girl on her shoulder. Then brushed the hair of the guy sitting next to her as he ran off, stage left. I could actually see him this time. I could make out some of the lapel on his jacket as he apparently stuck his head between the boy and girl and mugged at me. At least, three other children could see him as well.

It was pandemonium for a few minutes. Two of the youngest ones were clueless as to what was going on? They both jumped up and were frozen in place with shocked looks on their faces. I managed, somehow, to get the kids calmed down again and we continued rehearsal. I'm amazed that they did calm down after all of that.

A few minutes later I saw him again as he ran back towards the dressing rooms. I had gone up on stage to give notes and he was still hanging around stage left. When I came up on stage he spooked again and the boy, who was off stage that way, jumped up and screamed. He could see every detail and described him as being around thirty, wearing a tweed jacket, cabby hat and slacks. All I could see was a pair of transparent pants and some dark blobs as he ran. We all could hear his footfalls as he ran back towards the dressing rooms. Much to my surprise, three of the kids jumped right up and ran after him. I stayed behind to calm the cast.

After a couple of minutes, the ghost chasers returned to the stage. When I asked if they had found him, they told me they had found him in the backstage costume loft, hiding way in the back corner of the room. The girl that took off after him said "He's not evil, just trying to get attention.". The attitude of some of these kids amazed me! Of the dozen or so that were there, four of us could see him. So now I believe in ghosts and or spirits, whatever you'd like to call them? I'm glad I wasn't there alone. There were other witnesses to confirm this extraordinary event. It was not a glitch in my brain. I saw what I saw and so did they. Or, at least, three others did.

The sensitive young lady he touched saw a cloudy dark blob. I saw her watching him walk up the middle isle and then her eyes followed him as he went behind her. Later, she saw a black cat up near the lighting. As soon as she brought my attention to the cat and I looked, she said it came down the curtain and left.

The ghost ran when I inadvertently approached him. That was the other thing that puzzled me? I wonder why he runs away from me? He avoids me like the plague.

The boy, who described him in detail, arrived early to rehearsal one day and had to wait outside for me. When I arrived, he told me he had heard laughing children from inside the building and they were imploring him to come inside and play. He said he got so creeped out that he moved from waiting in front of one door to another on the other side of the building.

Why couldn't all of us see every detail? Was I now seeing him because I was experiencing and believing in metaphysical things? I wondered if the crystal heart I received and will discuss in the next chapter, imparted some power of perception in me?

I don't know why the playhouse has become so active, in the haunted sense, within the last few years. We have regular anomalous occurrences now. During the fall 2018 production, I was there alone cleaning and preparing for that night's final dress rehearsal. I was standing on stage right when I looked up at the light booth and saw the spot light we had borrowed. I often talk out loud to myself, especially when I'm on stage and with dramatic effect I declared, "Tonight, we are adding a spotlight." Right after saying that, the bank of lights that were lighting my section of the stage increased in intensity. It made me laugh, for Oscar, as we call him, is a prankster. I asked if he would like to do the lights that night and would he lower the intensity back down, please? I got no reply and had to go up and lower them myself.

That grand old haunted playhouse inspired me to write a musical in its honor called, Haunted Hannan Playhouse. While I was on stage directing the fall 2018, production of Haunted Hannan Playhouse, one young lady screeched and jumped, telling me that she had just been touched by an unseen spirit. On a whim, I asked her if she was a sensitive? She replied, "Yes, ever since I can remember." She told me it was okay and that she wasn't afraid of Oscar. She got touched on the hair during another rehearsal. It seems spirits may be able to read our aura's and can single out the sensitives? The one Oscar touched in the fall of 2017 was also a sensitive.

During those same rehearsals, I heard a word that's used in the play we were rehearsing come out of a speaker from a system that was turned off. The male voice said "Smores!" I was right below the speaker at the time and quickly looked up on stage to see if anyone else heard it? I was the only one and was very disappointed by that. A very weird thing to have happened, but I'm sure it was not a glitch in my brain. The play I was directing at the time is another one I wrote called, Camp Pleasant Trees. That made me wonder about the word smores? It is a recently invented word that Oscar would never have heard during his physical life on earth, but was in the play. Perhaps that is why Oscar thought it so funny?

According to a sensitive, Oscar was murdered at the playhouse when it was still under construction. He was shot and fell to the floor where the back of the seating is and near that speaker that exclaimed, "smores!" He fell to the ground somewhere near where he was watching the rehearsal from the night of the sighting. Quite often, over the years, I've had people come from the area near the light booth or below the light booth and ask me if the playhouse was haunted? I always replied, "Some think so." Now I'm a solid member of those who think so. When people ask me that question now it is a quick reply of "Yes, very!". Recently, I bought an EMF (electromagnetic field detector) and took it to the playhouse. The one place it went off was near the light booth.

During a performance once, Oscar hit a sound queue without the sound person touching the queue button. He's manipulated the lights on at least three different occasions and once during a live performance. During one performance, the kids said they could hear him laugh in the next dressing room while they were joking around in the big dressing room. The rooms are divided by a curtain hung over the door and an opening at the ceiling level, so it's easy to hear any noise coming from that small dressing room. I asked them what his laugh sounded like and they said, "yours!". Huh?

One day I heard what sounded like children running around upstairs. It was the first rehearsal for a high school production, in March of 2019. The teens had just started to arrive for their first rehearsal and I asked the students who had gone upstairs? They shrugged their shoulders, so I went to see for myself. They are not supposed to mess with any costumes or props that they don't use and I was going to lay down the law. When I went to see for myself there was nobody there? So, I smiled and said "hello?" no reply came. Upstairs a picture of a black blob was taken by a wildlife camera that was left over night.

At least four ghost hunting crews have been in the playhouse. One of them said there are a total of eight entities there. They asked the ghosts questions, utilizing their instruments and found that they like the plays. A sensitive member of our play group told me that one entity is a polish girl. She said the Polish girl didn't die there, but had a sentimental attachment to the building. The playhouse was a Polish hall from 1912 until it was bought by the Willapa Players in the sixties.

Another spirit is a costumer, so I was told. I have been haunting that playhouse personally for over thirty-five years and knew a lot of the old timers who have passed. I believe the costumer might be someone I did a lot of theater with, named Wilma. I asked an old timer who she thought the costumer might be and she came up with Wilma, as well.

In the fall of 2019, I was sitting in the front row when a girl's voice whispered something in my ear. Another lady in that play was sitting in the same seat and heard laughter from a little girl behind her during another rehearsal. Prior to that I and another cast member heard laughter emanate from an alcove that is adjacent to the seating area. When I heard it, I looked and saw the curtains retreat a little, as if someone had backed off.

Ghosts are such a mystery. How do they retain their existence for so long? Why are they stuck at a particular location, or are they stuck? How is it that Oscar learned, "smores!", a new and unique word for him? Why are they active some of the time and not all of the time? What is their schedule? What made the playhouse become so mystically and overtly active all of the sudden?

Another, very strange incident, happened to me at the playhouse in September of 2018 as I arrived to open the playhouse for that night's rehearsal. As I approached the door, I saw an old, unusual crow, sitting on the power line very near me. I believe I could see some kind of small colorful ribbon or something tied to his leg? He appeared a little dirty and his feathers didn't shine like the other crows. I said "Hello, how are you?" and started in the door when I heard a voice. The playhouse is somewhat isolated on the end of town and there was no one around. The voice sounded cartoonish and like it was coming from the bottom of a barrel. My first instinct told me it was outside the building, but I quickly assumed it must be Oscar talking from inside the building, so I jumped into the lobby asking "What did you say?" I heard nothing.

It wasn't until later that night I came up with the theory that it was the crow who talked to me. I couldn't quite understand the four or five-word sentence that was uttered. It was something like "I'm watching out for you."? Or "I'm watching over you."?

Since that incident I haven't seen that crow again. There is a murder of crows that frequent that area and I feed them nuts and raisins when they're around. I feel they know me and I like them and respect them. They are very clever and resourceful and very beautiful with their jet-black plumage. I look for that old crow every time I visit the playhouse, which is often and I haven't seen him since.

I posted a story about this incident on Facebook and of all people, my sister Teri replied that she too had heard a crow talk once. All it said was "hello". That occurred in Naselle Washington, which lies about forty miles south of Raymond. Then other stories showed up on the posting about known talking crows here and there. So, evidently, it's not that uncommon. Who knew?

Why am I writing about a haunted playhouse and talking crows? Because I now believe it is all connected. There is a reason mystical events have peaked at the playhouse. I believe it might have to do with me? Since I have been engaged with the forest people, I have witnessed many strange and wonderous experiences. Was that crow sent to me? I can't say for sure, but I do believe it is was. Have I become some kind of catalyst for metaphysical events? Also, very probable?

I went from skeptic with an open mind to believing in UFO's, Ghosts and sasquatch, all within about two years. Yikes! How could that possibly be true!? Fortunately, I have had plenty of witnesses that were with me for all three. That informs me it isn't just a glitch in my brain and I'm not cray cray. Unless all of my friends and family are?

CHAPTER 5

The Woo

THESE DAYS IT is not uncommon to find a chapter, or at least a few paragraphs in a book about sasquatch that addresses the woo, as its most commonly called. If I had finished writing this book in 2016, this chapter wouldn't be in it. I actually started getting suspicious that the rumors of Woo might be true way back in 2012. I began to experience very synchronistic events. What took me so long to become a believer? I was busy clinging to my cultural denial system, without even being aware of it.

I remember one day hiking along and thinking to myself that it was nice that sasquatch had the area across that big creek to themselves. Immediately after thinking that I heard a big branch snap across the creek, as if to say, "Yes, we like it over here." Other incidents like that one kept coming.

How was it I saw a sasquatch up close on the very first trip near that creek Connie told me about? It seemed too coincidental. Especially considering the first four years when there had been no hint that they even existed, other than one possible print.

Had I become that good, or did they all know me now and decide that I was an okay homo sapien sapien to interact with? Perhaps, the word got out over the sasquatch social media? That could explain my good luck on finding so many new families in unique areas. They knew I was coming and waited for me to arrive. I was wondering how that social network worked?

One day I called my friend Johnny Manson, the organizer for the Quinault Sasquatch Summit and he asked if I could fill in for a presenter that couldn't make it for his scheduled appearance on opening night. I agreed to do it with only two days to gather some kind of presentation together. I strung several minutes of my videos together and then decided my best bet was just to wing it and keep telling stories. I am sure I irked some of the main presenters off when I said that anyone exploiting bigfoot for personal or financial gain was not helping the cause. I didn't mean people couldn't make money off of art, movies, presentations or books about sasquatch. I just have a problem with wanton greed and exploitive arrogance. My mouth has a way of not properly articulating my true thoughts sometimes.

I also told that audience of around a thousand people, that I hadn't experienced any woo in connection with sasquatch. I was suspicious that I had, but I kept it to myself because, you know, the denial thing. I did mention that I'd seen quite a few UFO's and that had me wondering if there was a connection? I managed to fill around 35 minutes before I began to lose momentum and Johnny rescued me with the hook.

About three weeks before that summit I received a gift, from the one I now call my teacher, of a large, heart shaped yellow crystal. I believed the gift was given to me as both a reward and a gesture of affection. I had been hiking up to a peak that had a stump with a large stone on it. I suspected the stone was of sasquatch origin, so I would leave a smaller rock alongside that stone as a representation of me. I also created a smiley face on another stump. Every time I would hike up to that spot and leave a stone, or glyph, it was cast off and that large stone remained. I thought that maybe the wind was blowing them off, so I put larger stones on the stump. With the exception of that one stone, they all would get knocked off and finally completely disappear. Then one day I hiked up there and I heard a call. It sounded so human and yet why would a human be up there yelling like that? I got the impression that the call was pleading with me. I came to the conclusion that I was being asked not to mess with that rock. From then on, I left it alone.

I realized that it was very important to him and might even be a memorial for someone dear to him. So, I paid my respects to it. The next time out I received the yellow crystal heart.

They understand much of our symbolism, including the heart shape. I have read and seen photos of hearts given to humans by sasquatch. I see it as a representation of their tender hearts. One man from upper Ontario told me they saved his son. He was home watching his son and fell asleep on the couch. Suddenly he was wide awake and in a panic! He took a quick look around and noticed the front door was wide open. He ran outside and called for his son. His son was quite close to a cliff that is on their property and could have fallen to his death. After that, he said they would receive gifts of heart shaped stones periodically. He knew immediately who woke him up. He had received a metaphysical wake-up call from the forest people and it saved his son!

The day I received the gift of the crystal heart I was hiking along with a fisherman who peeled off for a fishing hole. Just a few hundred yards and around a corner, the crystal was lying on the road. I first spotted it fifty yards off and wondered what it was? As I got closer, I began to think it might be a piece of jell? I was almost on top of it before I realized what it was. I picked it up and got very emotional. Instantly,

I knew it was a very special gift for me. It was amazing and absolutely gorgeous even though it was a little dirty at the time. As I stood there I could hear talking out in the woods. It sounded like two males. The trees weren't that thick, but I couldn't see anyone? I held the gifted heart to my heart and thanked my gift givers out loud. I was overwhelmed by their generous and gorgeous gift. I still am. The heart measures almost four and a half inches across.

It felt very special, to have them give such a great and meaningful gift to me. That was the moment I began to believe we were forming a special connection. It was no longer me researching them and trying to study their interactions, collecting evidence and so on. It had become a friendship, a relationship. I can't begin to describe what it is like to be accepted in such an earnest and deep way by them. I felt like they had become my very close friends and special family. No longer did I give a damn about collecting evidence. I turned off all of my electronics and wouldn't turn them on again for almost two years.

I told my friends and family about the crystal and asked a few I thought might have an answer? I was told by two or three people to meditate with it and that would help form a psychic connection with the forest people. As usual, I was a bit skeptical, but I decided to keep an open heart.

The next time I hiked that road I heard something move behind me at the same location I received the crystal heart. I turned and I saw nothing, yet, I knew someone was right there. Again, I thanked them for that extraordinary gift.

It seems over the course of this extended metaphysical life adventure that I receive messages over and over until I get it. Those who are guiding me are very patient. Around this time, when I shared a story, I began hearing from random people that I was chosen. I rejected such a crazy notion. Chosen? By whom? Why? What could they want me for? People who don't know each other were telling me that. Again, denial system made me reject that notion, even though I was hearing it over and over again. So much so it made me wonder what was going on?

I was even told a couple of times that I was to become a shaman, or that my life was shamanistic. I bought a couple of books on the subject of shamanism and was surprised to find out that almost all were chosen and did not choose to become a shaman. At this writing I still do not consider myself a shaman or even a shaman in training. I don't reject it either. The origin of the word shaman comes from south central Siberia. It essentially means someone who has esoteric metaphysical knowledge and interacts with spirits.

At this juncture I thought it was only about friendship and nothing more. I leave them gifts and play music for them and because of that they like me and I like them, nothing more. I now think that might have been a little bit of wishful thinking. I already knew that something was up. I just didn't know what?

Meanwhile, the receiving of the crystal heart reminded me of another strange stone I had found decades before. It is very unusual, with a crystal embedded in agate that fits in the palm of my hand. It also appears to have been subjected to heat as it shows some vitrification. Small circles that appear on the surface were possibly caused by a rain of small hot spherical objects, which I believe might be from a meteoric explosion? I had found it after a storm washed it out of an embankment. I could tell it had been worked by human hands, but I didn't really look at it very carefully. I was puzzled about its function? It was too small to be a native fish net weight. I did notice what looked like a face on it, but I really didn't look at it that carefully and thought my brain might be suffering from pareidolia? I didn't know why, but I felt it was very important, so I hid it in my house. I live alone. Who was I hiding it from?

I would pull it out once in a while and hold it. It's very smooth and I liked the way it felt in my hand. But I never really took a close look at it. The carvings are so small they alluded my attention.

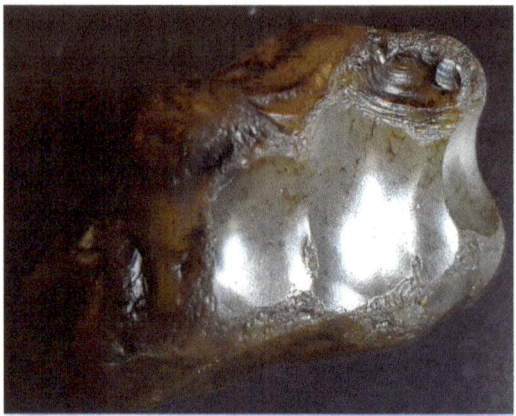

You can see a representation of a flying saucer and two planets tucked up above in the upper right corner. On the left upper left part of the saucer something appears to be emanating?

To me this looks like an ET with a feather on his forehead.

After receiving and finally accepting my instruction to meditate with the crystal heart I remembered the agate and took it out of its hiding place. I was suddenly so fascinating by that gorgeous stone, I spent two days examining it. I was stunned to see a water fall with a pool, a sleeping wolf, moose head, whale, illuminated spirit and a perfect representation of a flying saucer with two planets carved next to it and two faces. There is also one that looks like a jelly fish, maybe? All of these carvings are very small and intricate, which is why I didn't notice them. The water fall, which is crystal, ends in a crystal pool surrounded by the darker agate. It's so well done! There even is yellow foam at the top of the water fall, represented by yellow crystal. It also has ninety-degree, perfect inside cuts down to the pool below the waterfall. I have no idea how those cuts or carvings could have been achieved with primitive tools? The two faces are really ingenious and best observed in low light conditions at an angle, such as a campfire. One face looks like an ET to me, with a feather on its forehead. A feather on a forehead is commonly known as a symbol for the third eye. If the stone is turned upside down, the face then reminds me of a sasquatch (hard to visualize in the above picture).

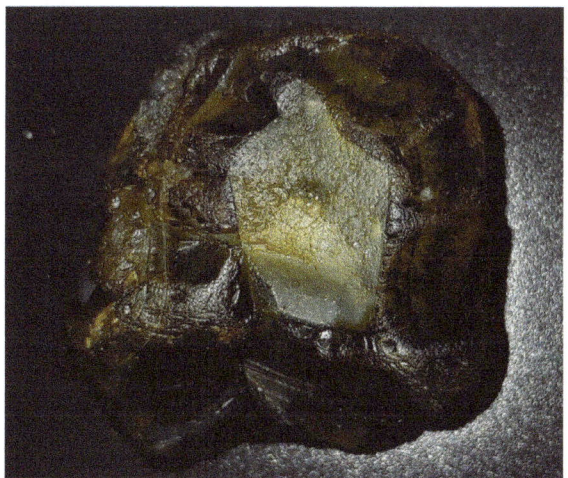

Pictured is the glowing figure. Note the indentation at the location of the heart. This figure, when viewed at a shallower angle, then appears as a waterfall with the pool at the bottom of the glowing figure.

I found the shaman stone fit in my right hand perfectly, as if it was made for me. It even has notches for my fingers. When I hold the stone in this manner the glowing spirit is visible in the palm of the hand. If held another way, the spirit is covered and only the UFO appears between the thumb and fingers. I have decided that the artist/shaman must have been right-handed. If held in the left hand the spirit or angel, is covered and the moose head is exposed. When I meditate, I hold it in my right hand with the spirit exposed at the palm.

It is interesting to note that there are no moose in this part of the country anymore and probably haven't been for thousands of years. The nearest moose are a couple of hundred miles away. Either this artifact is old enough to have been carved when moose were still inhabiting this area, or it came from where moose are currently indigenous. I believe the former, because of the whale and the other carving that might be a jelly fish show evidence that it was probably manufactured locally. So, therefore I believe it is thousands of years old.

I am now convinced that I was meant to find the stone. In the 1980's I dreamt of a visitation in my room by an insect like being who reminded me of a praying mantis. I told my sister Sonja and Mom about it, because it seemed so real and detailed. In my dream I woke up to this being in my room and I freaked, jumped up out of bed, grabbed my guitar and started swinging at the creature. He had the demeanor of being in a light mood, while he danced and avoided my swings with deft skill. That is all of the dream I remember. A few days or weeks later I was standing at the island counter in my parent's kitchen when my sister slams a book down in front of me. On the cover of the book is the face of the praying mantis being I saw in my dream. I got a huge chill, of course. On the cover of the book Communion, by Whitley Schreiber, the alien is wearing the same smirk I remembered from my dream. It was around this time, perhaps in the late 80s, when I found the shaman stone.

The first time I meditated with these two gifts, I held the heart to my chest with my left hand the shaman stone in my right hand. After about ten minutes I became sleepy and rolled over on my right side. My cat came in and jumped up on my bed and began to curl up next to me, behind my knees. That prompted, whatever was hovering above me, to slam against my bedroom wall knocking over a zero-gravity chair that was folded up and leaning against it. My cat scrambled off the bed and out of the bedroom. I got an adrenaline rush and jumped out of bed, turned the lights on and cussed at whatever that thing was. I was mad, because it scared my cat and I screamed in my head not to do that again, or else! Or else what? I kind of laugh at that now. What was I going to do about it?

I perceived the entity, or spirit, as a dark, smoky cloud. My eyes were closed until it hit the wall and exited the room, yet I saw it with my third eye.

All of those years that stone had sat in my roll top desk just waiting for me to release the genie. It could be that genie was in the crystal heart, I'm not sure? Whatever the case, I now believe it was not an evil entity. My reasoning is that sasquatch would protect me from anything evil popping out of their gift. The shaman stone may have been separated from its owner when a massive earthquake at a subduction zone off the coast of Washington caused a huge tsunami in the year 1700? Did the shaman decide to spirit jump into the stone when he or she saw the tsunami coming? This, of course, is wild speculation. It is also the way my brain processes information now days. I'm no longer tethered to our generally accepted reality and so-called logical explanations.

I had a few other incidents and then I asked the advice of my friend, Eryn. Her advice was to cleanse them. She told me to take my artifacts up to a certain, strong metaphysical, secret location. Per her instruction, I utilized a circular rock enclosure in the shallow water of a river and immersed my artifacts in the circle. I beat my drum and sang to the spirits in the mountains. I then placed my hands on a tree and said a prayer that I hoped would lead the spirit back to nature.

I talked to three people about this sacred, powerful area, before I went, not mentioning its power. It is near a popular camping area. Unsolicited, I received three strange stories about that area. One lady told me she was sitting at a picnic table when a small fairy came and hovered in front of her face for a moment," just like a humming bird!", then took off and disappeared. She said she was shocked by that event.

Another lady was hiking to a lake with her grandson when he suddenly told her he saw himself peeking at him from behind a tree. Then, a bit later in the hike, while crossing a bridge, he saw himself again in a dry creek bed staring at him. Then another friend told me she had been spotlighted by a UFO at night in that same area. So, I got the impression it was the place to go.

When I mentioned to those few I was going there, I did not ask about metaphysical experiences. It turned out everyone had a story to tell and were willing to tell me. That is the kind of synchronicity I often experience. I talk to three people about taking a trip to a certain location and they are all familiar with it and have a bizarre story to tell.

I completed my ceremony and I believe I released that entity? I've had other anomalous events occur, those are probably centered around the crystal heart or my house. How do I know this? I don't know for certain? I have just become more accustomed to trusting my instincts, because they seem to be correct so often. My instincts have always been good, it's just that I haven't always trusted them. Now I attempt to pay attention to them at all times.

For about eighteen months after receiving the heart, my hands would shoot out blue dielectric light during and after handling it. It was quite a show as the blue light arced here and there. I couldn't feel it at all, like you can with white static electricity. There was no popping or stinging. Most often I would see it in the morning before dawn as I woke up. I would reach for my eye glasses and the blue light would emanate from my fingers and connect to my glasses a few inches before I touched them.

Unfortunately, I became obsessed with a couple of projects of mine and lapsed in my meditation routine for about a year. I believe that heart could possibly have been injected with some kind of power and I failed to take full advantage of it? It might have been infused with information that was important? Some of the power it possessed had a shelf life. The blue light slowly disappeared until all I see now is a little white static electrical build up once in a while. I'm sure there is still plenty of information and power left in that crystal. It might be a communication device, or a hard drive of sorts. The question is whether I will ever gain the ability to access it? It could also be that the blue discharge was loaded in the crystal and ran down like a battery. Was it added as an additional amusement for me? A sort of parlor trick? It was very amusing and fascinating.

I have had some other, very strange, occurrences since I started meditating with those powerful objects. In fact, I had extreme static electricity recently, but it was white and didn't arc like the blue light. However, just the other morning, I touched my cat when I woke up and thought I saw a little blue.

I began to hear sharp, loud noises, just before I fell asleep and they would bring me back to wide awake. The sounds seemed random. I would hear a whistle blow or a bell ring or a voice that went "HA!". I had no idea what it was about? I thought it was probably just a noise in my head and not external. Then I had my friend Russell Wilson and his girlfriend at the time, stay over at my house for a couple of nights. I gave my bed up to them and I slept in the music room on the floor. I was lying on my left side on a mattress on the floor when I heard a very loud electronic sound behind my head. I rolled over, but saw nothing? The room was all turned off and completely dark. The next morning, I told Russell about it and he asked, "Yeah, what was that noise?". I was surprised the noise was external and also a bit relieved. So why the random noise? I now believe they were attempting to show me the sweet spot for my meditation. When I begin to fall asleep, they would sound the alarm to let me know I was drifting past the sweet spot.

The sweet spot would be when my brain is producing theta waves, which occur between 3 to 8 HZ. Regular awake frequencies are between 12 to 38 HZ, which are called beta waves. Theta waves are the gateway to learning, memory and intuition.

Russell told me he heard something unusual coming from my room the next night as well. He got up to go to the bathroom at around 2:30 in the morning and heard a strange hum, like a generator, coming from my room. Again, nothing in the room was turned on.

Not that long ago I was still hearing sounds like some kind of alarm for an electronic device come from one of my rooms. If I get up to trace it, it will cease to make noise and that prevents me from finding out where the noise is emanating from? That is while I'm awake, on the couch. The noises that I heard just before drifting off to sleep have almost ceased, but still continue sporadically.

I also was guided to, what I'm sure, is a meteorite. I was watching a program on the Chelyabynsk Meteor one night. Meteorite hunters were picking up meteorites in Russian farm fields. The region was snow covered when the bolide exploded and it created holes in the crusted snow where the vitrified pieces from that disintegration hit the ground. All they had to do was go peer down a hole in the snow and there one would be.

While watching the program I had the thought that I would like to find a meteorite someday. The next morning, I went hiking way up the Skokomish river. I was standing on a rocky shoreline taking a break before hiking back out. Standing there, I was admiring the gorgeous view when I looked down at the rocky shoreline of ancient, grey sandstone. Lying between my feet, on top of the light grey ancient sand stone river rock, was a jet-black object. As soon as I saw it, I knew it was something unusual. In fact, I already knew what it was. I picked it up and immediately knew my first impression was correct. It looked just like the meteorites they were finding on the program the night before. It is pitch black, about the size of a large marble and vitrified. It is also very heavy for its size. I believe it is most likely iron nickel and is magnetic. I can pick it up with a cow magnet. I haven't had it checked to be sure but, for myself, I don't need to have it checked. I know what it is. There are only three kinds of rock in the Olympics, shale, sandstone and basalt. Basalt would be the most ferrous among them and slightly magnetic, but basalt cannot be picked up with a cow magnet.

I will trust my instincts on this one and believe it to be a meteorite. It was my first lesson in something other than telepathy. They, subconsciously, guided me to it. Or, maybe they could look into the future and see exactly where I was going to stand when I took a break from my hike? Or, as one of my friends told me, I manifested it. Another thing I've heard from others when I've related one of my miraculous stories.

I have found the more I meditate, the more I can remember my dreams. One night I dreamt I saw a school bus picking up children at a dead-end road. As the bus turned around, I noticed an adult male sasquatch going behind it. I was thinking that nobody saw him but me and how crazy is that!? As the bus came by, I took a look inside and had eye contact with a very young female sasquatch. She had a gentle, pleasant face and was riding the bus as if she was going to school. I looked back at the sasquatch and he was just standing there smiling at me. I walked up to the smiling, tall sasquatch and shook his hand. His grip was so strong it woke me up. It wasn't like waking up from a regular dream. This one seemed so real that I was surprised to see I was in bed.

I interpret that dream as my introduction to a sasquatch father and daughter who live near town. The school bus, perhaps, signified school? I now believe that father is my teacher. My other thought about the dream is that they would like to be thought of as more human.

I'm sure it was not his real face. It was like a morphed Harry and the Henderson's kind of face and body, just not as comical. I believe the similarity to Harry was a device to put me at ease.

I know he is the one who gave me the gift of the heart shaped crystal. I also believe it was spiritual interaction and not a dream. My friend and teacher was introducing himself and his daughter to me.

I knew there was a young one up there, because I'd seen sign of her playing in the top of an alder tree. Another tree nearby had a large log lodged in it about ten feet up. That log appeared after I called out a few days before, because I was suspicious there might be some sasquatch living in that area?

The five to six-foot-long and five or six-inch-thick log appeared around 2014, three years before my hand shake dream. The dream left me wondering about the mother? Was she gone? Is that who the rock on the stump memorializes?

One day, in the year 2018 I came down from paying my respects to the rock memorial and the center of the road was strewn with daisies for several yards. I'm pretty sure that was a show of affection from the daughter, who I call Candace.

CHAPTER 6

My Awakening

BEFORE I FOUND the meteorite, I decided to conduct some experiments to confirm my suspicion that they are telepathic and that we had connected on that level? My first experiment was hiking out to where the one I call Mr. Ed hangs out and asked in my head for a vocal? I immediately heard what sounded like a human calling from quite far away and barely audible. I was suspicious of what I was hearing because of the timing. Why would I hear a human now, right after I ask for a vocal in my head? Then I realized the call was coming closer. In fact, he was moving at a rate that could not be human. I remembered hearing that voice once before. It was the voice that was calling to me as I stood by the possible memorial. It was also coming from that general direction. I believe now it was my teacher. I purposely picked Mr. Ed because I wanted to hear what he sounded like? Instead, my teacher came from his territory and vocalized. I have heard Mr. Ed since though. I marked off the first experiment as passed. I thanked him in my head for the vocal and he immediately stopped vocalizing.

I don't have a name for my teacher, other than, teacher or the shaman of the woods. I have a few friends who can hear them through mind speak and know the names of their forest people friends. I would love to know my teachers name?

Mr. Ed. Is a sasquatch loner, just outside of town. I have left him gifts at two different locations. One of those locations he left me a live mouse. I was hiking back down from the gifting location when I encountered a mouse sitting still in the middle of the road, watching me approach. I stopped and asked the mouse "Why are you just sitting there?" He just stared back at me with his cute little eyes. I took a closer look and could see that his hind legs were twisted and broken. I knew then that he was presented as a gift, but I don't eat live mice, so I left him there. The next two times I went up there Mr. Ed pushed a tree down in the distance. I felt bad that he was angry at me for not taking the gift. Since then, we're good again. He now understands why I don't eat live mice. He even left me a colorful and interesting cairn to let me know he was cool with me again.

The cairn in the above photo was left on a gifting stump where I would leave apples and other goodies for Mr. Ed.

I believe I might have heard Mr. Ed looking through rock piles for rodents in a local quarry in early 2020. I had come to the entrance of the quarry and I could hear rocks being moved around on the far side, which is obscured by other rock piles and young alder trees. I listened for a while and then I tried to get to a position where I might be able to see. It was impossible to move closer without being detected. As soon as I made a noise the sound stopped and whatever was over there left. I'm pretty sure it wasn't a bear. If it was Mr. Ed, he had gotten so distracted by his quest that he had not detected me entering the quarry. I believe he was hunting for rodents. Sometimes, they make mistakes.

One hot summer day at that same quarry I got the impression that I shouldn't enter it. So, I turned around and began to hike out. After about a hundred yards of hiking I heard a big crash come from the quarry, as if to say," Your impression was correct and thank you for turning around and leaving." There is a natural pool that is fed by a spring on the far side of that quarry where I had heard the rocks being moved around. I figure Mr. Ed and possibly others might have been cooling off, didn't feel like moving and knew I was coming. So, he sent me a message to turn around and hike out.

About a year later I was standing at the entrance of that quarry thinking about that day and my ability to sense what to do. As I was standing there, I heard a whoop from the ridge above the quarry. Mr. Ed was letting me know that he could hear me thinking about that event and was acknowledging it. That maybe the only time I've heard a vocal from Mr. Ed.

A few months later, up in the Olympics I came upon, what appeared to be a drunk mouse. He was staggering in the middle of the trail and I was immediately suspicious that he was also a gift. I walked along side of him and gave him encouragement as he slowly recovered. I kept looking around for a sasquatch, but saw none. He finally was healthy enough to start grazing after about thirty yards of travel down the trail. I bid him good day and good luck and went on my way. They now know that I don't eat live mice. They mostly gift me feathers these days. I love the feathers.

How did they make that second mouse stagger like that? I thought at the time, they might have thumped the top of its head until it was about to get knocked out? Then, someone told me they might have done it with infra sound? I think that sounds like a more plausible explanation of why it recovered so quickly and completely.

These days I often receive pristine dead moles in my teacher's territory. They always look very fresh. The one in the picture below was left just a few minutes before I arrived. I know this because a pickup truck drove this road less than an hour before I came through. The mole was lying in the tire track of the road and the driver probably wouldn't have noticed it among all the other debris and therefore would not have avoided running over it. So far this calendar year I've seen around half a dozen gifted moles. Most of the time I receive them on the loop I hike to the memorial.

There might be some sort of metaphorical meaning to this particular gift. A furry animal that lives under ground? Mole fur is really nice, by the way.

For one of my telepathic experiments, I took a small yellow crystal I had found and hid it on the stump Mr. Ed built the cairn on. I even covered the crystal with bark and pieces of wood so it wasn't visible. Then I sent a message that it was there. The next time I went out there and checked, it was gone. I did that experiment two more times, several miles away in another sasquatch family's territory. Both those times I peeled back some moss and placed the crystal under the moss. Then I groomed it so you couldn't tell there was anything under the moss. I then took a mental picture of it and sent that image and location to them. At both locations, the crystals were gone when I went back to check.

One day, during the series of telepathic experiments I went skiing at White Pass, Washington. As I was driving back, I got an idea for another experiment. I sent a message to those living in a particular area known for sightings. I asked them to leave something along the highway that I was familiar with and could see on my drive back home. I almost forgot about my request when on the side of the highway, coming down an embankment, I recognized a sasquatch track line right in the general area I was targeting. The tracks were in perfect line and at the right stride of a sasquatch coming down a slope, right next to the highway! I thought about turning around and examining them. But I had no camera or phone with me and I didn't want to draw attention to them, so I just kept going. Again, I thanked them in my head. I wonder to this day if anyone in the know saw the track line and understood what they were looking at?

A few weeks after I began the experiments, I got a request from Russell Wilson to find a family closer to where he lives in Centralia Washington. I told him we could try, but I wasn't that optimistic? I picked Russell up before dawn on Labor Day morning, 2017. We began randomly driving around the general region looking for evidence in the woods of some sort of sasquatch activity.

After about two hours of cruising around I noticed an area, adjacent to the gravel road we were on, where it looked like juveniles had been playing. It was a young mixed patch of woods. There were many small, bent trees in every direction and some other things that looked suspicious. I stopped the car and told Russell to take a look and he agreed that it looked very suspicious (The trees pictured below is not of that particular patch of woods, but more obviously illustrates some of what they do.).

Most people can't tell the difference from a natural gnarled patch of woods and one that's been used as a playground for juvenile sasquatch. Our experienced eyes could see it. A little bit further we came upon, what was a possible sasquatch structure (picture of structure below). We stopped and started to investigate. After a while Russell detected something moving and making noise in an adjacent patch of trees. I quickly walked closer to that area and jumped up on a stump to get a better look. There was no wind, yet I could see a fern was swaying dramatically and could hear something crawling down the hill on the other side of the berm from us. I ran closer and jumped up on another stump to see what was over there? As I looked down, what I believe was an old abandoned road, I could see something sticking up above the shadow of a fallen tree. It appeared to be a cinnamon-colored tuft of hair. Below that tuft of hair was a dark blob on the edge of that abandoned road. I was straining my eyes to understand what I was looking at when I started to ask Russell if he could see what I was seeing? Then that tuft of hair showed what it was attached to when the young male sasquatch scrambled into some brush and out of sight. I immediately jumped off the stump and found a limb to knock with. I knocked and the juvenile quickly knocked back. I then left him a gift of a cliff bar and some nuts and told him that I hoped we could come back sometime and play music for them.

Several months later we would be standing next to that structure again and I was demonstrating to Russell their telepathic abilities. I asked for a knock, telepathically and we got one immediately. It was way off in the distance and came so quickly it was as if he knew what I was going to ask, which he did. After that we worked our way close to some woods and we could hear what we assumed, was the young male we had seen on Labor Day. He was very close, but I couldn't see him? Then I heard the patriarch start to call way off in the distance. Russell couldn't tell it was a sasquatch at first. He was interpreting the calls as some sort of machinery. So, the local patriarch kept calling while coming towards us until Russell realized he was hearing a sasquatch and not machinery. I thanked the forest person for his vocals through mind speak and he immediately stopped vocalizing. I was happy to have a witness along for the sixth and final test.

This picture was taken just before Russell Wilson
detected the young male sasquatch.

It amazed me that they went to such extremes, just to prove to me that they are telepathic. Why? Am I that important to them? They recognize me where ever I go now. The experiments were proven to work with five different sasquatch families, spread out over western Washington. As I write this, I've interacted with sasquatch in four different states and over thirty different locations. All I have to do is camp out somewhere novel and almost every time some will come and vocalize to me. My heart soars every time I hear their greetings. It is the most amazing thing to know that they are calling to me and acknowledging our bond as special.

I now believe that our telepathic connection had been building before I received the gift of the crystal heart. The gift might have made that connection a little stronger? I also think they might have hoped it would make communication a two-way street? As of this writing and to my disappointment and perhaps theirs, that hasn't happened.

In my frustration to hear them through mind speak I began asking a few select friends if they knew where I might purchase a micro dose of LSD or something with DMT in it? I thought if I could take something psychedelic, maybe it would deliver me their mind speak. Finally, I gave up on that idea and backpacked up into the Olympics and tried something else. I smoked a bunch of cannabis and crawled into my tent. Jacques and crew came and vocalized to let me know they were right there.

I began to meditate and suddenly I felt a surge through my body. As I felt the surge, I went into an altered state of consciousness and journeyed. This happened at least three times for what seemed like just a few seconds each. I can only remember pieces of the last trip. I traveled to another dimension or spirit world. The flora was lush, colorful, smooth and waxy looking. There was a being with a large yellow round pleasant face, like the sun, who smiled and communicated with me. I don't remember what was communicated? I felt a wonderful peace beyond description. My journey was full of love and support and was a very positive experience.

I'm not sure what to make of what I saw on that last trip? It could be they were showing me things that they knew I would like and understand and was not reflective of their true reality. Perhaps their world would be too difficult to comprehend, if they showed me their true nature. Or, maybe it was the sun? There are those who believe that Gaia and the sun are actually conscious beings. I do believe I journeyed to other realms and did not hallucinate.

After my induced journey I was disappointed to learn that I still couldn't hear them through mind-speak. I was very thankful for the experience and canceled my search for psychedelics. It was a very pleasant, eye-opening experience. That journey experience is responsible for much of my evolution toward becoming spiritual. The other thing is, somehow, I knew that they would help me journey? That tells me that I do pick up on messages, even if they are subconscious.

How did they bring about the altered state of consciousness? I believe they induced DMT to be released from my body's natural reserves. DMT is naturally produced within the human body and can be found in the pineal gland, otherwise known, in some circles, as the third eye. DMT is known to be released upon death and sleep. I believe that is the surge I was feeling. I've come close to journeying many times without any assistance since that night. I've come up short so far. I know of shaman that can journey without the aid of any mind-altering substance. It is a rare gift and takes years of disciplined practice. Unfortunately, I'm not that disciplined.

I still have frustrations at not being able to hear them through mind speak. I have gained certain powers of perception, though. For instance, I always seem to know whether I'm dealing with a male or female sasquatch? I will get general impressions of the sasquatch that's lurking outside of my tent, or the gender of the owner of a print I've found. Later, it will turn out I was correct.

They also leave me sign posts to follow. Usually, two broken branches at the beginning of a road means "Go this way". When I see two breaks and follow them, they will leave a break every once in a while, along the way, to tell me I'm going in the right direction and haven't passed it yet. Finally, they will break several branches on a tree that gives me notice I'm close to something interesting. I know how these signs look and they are very specifically done. So, it's easy for me to tell the difference from weather or other ways branches might break.

In August of 2017 I followed some of their sign posts and it led me up into a deep cut valley in the Olympic mountains. When I found the location, I knew it was what they wanted me to find. It was a beautiful area between steep, basalt cliffs and nestled within old growth hemlock, cedar and Douglass fir. There were huge old trees there, a swimming hole, water fall and lots of interesting places for exploring.

I believe, while doing my first reconnaissance, I might have found another rodent trap at a rock slide. It was just a pile of rocks. To me it appeared to have been done on purpose. This would be in the Wynootchee valley and only a few miles away from the other rodent trap I found.

As I was checking out the place, I was slightly annoyed by the noise of a construction crew repairing the main road nearby. I knew they would knock off work by 4:00 P.M. As I was setting up camp mid-afternoon and before the road crew knocked off, I began to hear Jacque, Peter and C.C. They seemed very excited and were apparently not bothered by the close proximity of the road crew? They were calling from a bluff across the river. The road crew were taking a break and the machinery was turned off. I'm sure the road crew workers could hear them. My friends were loud and sounding like primates with their whoops. I just wonder what the road crew thought? My thought was "Yeah, I found it! It's nice!…What the Hell!? You really seem very excited for some reason?" I got the immediate impression it was more than just a greeting. It was a celebration!

I thought it strange that they came and vocalized with such enthusiasm with other humans close by? It seemed like it was a big step of some sort? Why were they so excited? I didn't get it? Later, it would slowly dawn on me that they had led me to the center of a regional vortex. I began seeing twisty trees around the campsite. It turns out that the center of a vortex is dead, like the eye of a hurricane. A regional vortex field has a substantial sized eye, so it was a false impression that the trees were twisty because of electromagnetism. But I had that impression or received that impression and it turned out to be correct. Knowing what I know now, I understand how important that was. For instance, when I was checking for distance and angles from the Montana House of Mystery, that location is intimately associated with those placements (This will be re-visited and explained in the chapter 8). It is with those distances and angles they proved I was led me to my home. It is also through math that they showed me my impression was correct and it was the center of a vortex field they led me to.

Lately, I have come to the realization that the whole idea was to get me to that location. It took them a few years to coax me there. I was not very adept at picking up on their queues at first.

CHAPTER 7

Bringing Family

I HAD TAKEN a few friends up with me to the Olympics camping and some of them had experiences. However, the forest people are particular. They are quiet as mice when I bring someone they don't want to interact with. I don't think they dislike these people, it's just that they know who they want me to bring, or under what circumstances they want them brought.

I've learned that they don't like alcohol, so I minimize that when I'm out there. Sometimes, I'll have a beer in the afternoon when I'm camping. Usually, that is after a hike and before nap time. Later in the evening I will almost always abstain. If there is too much alcohol being consumed it's likely they will shut down.

One night I brought a friend, who had some Irish whiskey. We had a few hard pulls on the flask, he more than I. I knew the trail was somewhat hazardous going back, so I got my friend heading back before he got too tilted. Then I realized that I had left my recorder back where we were sitting. I parked my friend where he was safe and went back to get the recorder. As I walked below a cliff, I heard a very big, lengthy fart. It stopped me in my tracks. I turned around and chuckled in the direction of his perch. It was too dark to see him, but judging from the sound, I could tell he was very close. I then continued to retrieve my recorder. I got a good laugh from the simulated fart, but I also realized that it was commentary. They have a way of mixing humor with a lesson. The next day, I climbed up to that perch and found some displaced moss where he had been sitting. It had an excellent view of the trail just a few feet below.

After that, I began to go camping alone and without alcohol. I started to hike more and back pack more. I would say it was kind of a cleansing. Not that they had any problem with my friend. It was the alcohol. But I also realized that it was time for the next step, although, I had no idea what that would be? I got the impression that it was time for me to go solo for a while.

In June of 2017, my great nephew Xander graduated from Carlsbad, California High School. I drove my Subaru forester down to attend his graduation and take him and his younger 15-year-old brother, Mason, on a road trip to their muumuu's house in Chinook Washington.

The first thing we did was drive straight and long up I-5 to station ourselves at the entrance of the redwoods for the next day. That was the worst part of the trip, because the heat was unbearable. Then we drove to Willow Creek the next day and camped at Bluff Creek camp ground that night.

When we entered the campground, there was no one there to check us in, so we picked a spot way in the back. I paid the attendant later. Mason set up a happy smile glyph on a stump near our camp and took a picture of it, so he could check for changes the next morning. Then we had a nice afternoon as I told them what I'd experienced and what to expect. Before it even got dark, we began to hear two vocalize with their owl call from the ridge above the camp. I'm not sure if the vocal they use is a specific pattern for me or if it's universal? I know many others hear them call in the same, or similar manner. Eight hundred-pound owls are what people in the know call them. I always tell everyone, when you hear them, you'll know. As soon as they started to call the nephews knew and both told me as much. It is a great honor to be presented with such a vociferous greeting.

They were only a couple of hundred yards up on a ridge adjacent to that famous campground. It is the same campground Patterson and Gimlin stayed at before they left to record the famous P/G film in 1967. When I camped with my great nephews there, the previous owner, who I met on an earlier expedition, was gone. He had finally sold the property after owning it since the early sixties. After they vocalized from the ridge it got quiet, as if they had to leave right away?

It was late in September, 2013 when I camped there with Russell Wilson. Russell and I heard a couple of branch breaks and a big thump after we got into our tents at night. Something had been thrown off that same hill adjacent to our campsite. I searched for that something the next day and did find a large, bowling ball sized rock that seemed out of place.

Now days, if I'm out and about during the day and they are close, I will hear a single knock or a branch break as a "hello", or I'll receive a gift of some kind. They do vocalize to me, at times, during the day, but it's rare. If I believe no humans are around, I sometimes knock or vocalize back.

The picture below was taken in 2013 as I stood next to the Klamath river and near the bigfoot highway and Bluff creek campground in northern California.

The next morning Mason checked on his glyph and it had been altered slightly. He had the picture on his phone from the night before for comparison. So, someone had come to visit that night? We then headed for O'Brian, Oregon via a lost highway that crosses the California/Oregon boarder tracking northwest from Happy camp, California, The location of the sculpture below.

After re-supplying in Happy Camp, we stopped on that lost highway for lunch on a pull off next to a hay field. A short time after we got back on the highway, we crossed a creek and standing in the creek bed, slowly moving toward us, was a ten-foot-tall sasquatch. He was about fifty yards or less away. I didn't think the nephews saw him, so I kept my mouth shut and kept driving. It would be two days later when Xander opened up about what he saw in northern California. I was ecstatic, "You saw him too! That's great!" Then we compared notes.

He was leaner than I would expect and yet still had those wide shoulders. His hair was cinnamon colored and to me his outline appeared to shimmer slightly on the edges. Xander didn't notice any shimmering. I am very thankful for his gift of a visual. Xander estimated he was about nine-foot-tall, while I estimated ten-foot-tall. Neither one of us could see his face, because it was shaded from the sun. I only saw him for about three or four seconds, but Xander got a real good look.

Watching the eye witness reports where they've taken measurements, people have a tendency to consistently under estimate their height. It might be due to their bulky bodies causing force perspective and making them appear shorter. I believe people under estimate their weight, as well.

I'm thinking the mature males are all over a thousand pounds, ...even the tiny ones.

Later that afternoon, we found a campground by a lake in southern Oregon. There were some other occupants close by at first, but by late afternoon we were the only ones left in our loop of the campground. As darkness fell, a couple of fishermen showed up on the lake. They anchored their boat straight across from where we were. As I was telling my nephews more stories, we started to hear bobcats going nuts in a hay field across the road from the campground. They were making all kinds of crazy vocalizations as they moved around the field. We were having fun listening to them and it went on for an amazing amount of time before it got quiet. That's when an adult male sasquatch vocalized from less than two hundred yards away. He was in the campground! As he began to vocalize, I stood up and faced that way and declared "That's a bigfoot!". The nephews already knew that. The fisherman tried to imitate the call. The nephews told me that it was so close and loud that it gave them a bit of an adrenaline rush. I felt that rush too. It is rare when I feel a rush like that. He was loud and not expected to be that close in a campground. Their vocals can do that to you when they catch you by surprise. I have told the sasquatch that I don't care about an occasional burst of adrenaline. To me, it's part of the fun. Also, I want to learn and I'm ready to feel fear in order for that to happen, if necessary.

The next day we traveled to northern Oregon to Spruce Run. We camped there for two nights and spent a whole day exploring. The first two nights we heard nothing. However, early on the second morning, as the other campers in that packed campground were fixing breakfast and coffee, a couple of sasquatch came to the ridge above our campsite and began to vocalize. I was shocked that they would do that, but then upon inspection of the other campers, I realized no one was paying attention. The adult humans all had their noses in their coolers, or were mixing the pancakes. There was one little girl who was looking in the direction of the ridge while attempting to imitate their call.

At the beginning of the trip, I had asked them to reveal themselves to my great nephews without scaring them. Besides one mild rush, I believe they succeeded very nicely.

I was happy to finally have someone to back me up when I tried to tell other family members of my adventures. After a while I asked Xander if he'd told his muumuu about seeing sasquatch? He said he had and I asked how she took it? "Not well." Was the answer. It used to irk me that she was so sure I was making a mistake in interpretation of my experiences, or I had lost my mind, or I was lying. Now, her weakened doubts make me laugh. In fact, her skeptical, pointed comments have pretty much disappeared.

The next month I had some other great nephews, a niece and their mother with me. All together there were five of us. We camped up in the Olympic National Park.

The first time I had camped there I had been looking for my forest friends Jacque, Peter and C.C. They had moved from where I had met them and I was trying to locate their new home. I camped in one valley and they didn't show up, so the next time I moved one valley over.

The night I found them, in the third valley, I felt like something was going to happen. I was in a national park campground full of campers. I still figured they would do something to let me know they were there, if they were there? It was about ten minutes after midnight when I heard a tree go down across the river. I was so happy I had found them and fell asleep with a big smile on my face.

The next morning, I got up and began fixing coffee and breakfast when I heard a chainsaw going. I quickly hiked over there to see what was going on? There were a couple of park rangers already cutting the log up. It had fallen across the trail. A couple of months later my forest friends pushed a tree down in the same area, but were careful to angle it so it didn't cross the trail. The tree was pretty good sized at over a foot wide at the base. The picture below is a section that's a third of the way up the tree where they cut a path for the trail.

I asked the ranger why the tree had fallen? He said "All trees are destined to fall sometime." This, by the way, was right below the cliff I would later hear that enormous fart.

I later found a place near the campground where I could hike for a few hundred yards into the woods at night and be in a private clearing. I took my great niece Ashlynn, her mother Sarah and three great nephews Hunter, Brian and Adrian there. Sasquatch seems to like that place. We set up our chairs and I could hear them around our perimeter. As we sat there, they slowly came in closer and closer from three sides until one made a twig snap, just a few feet behind Hunter. He jumped up and they all jumped up and immediately began getting ready to go. As they were folding their chairs up in haste, I was telling everyone to calm down and said "They are just curious and want to get a closer look." My relatives had enough and it was time to go. They were all slightly freaked. I believe now the one that made that twig crack was the juvenile I call Alice. That night, right after we retired to our tents, they vocalized from a distance. My great niece Ashlynn and her mother Sarah heard them and that made me happy.

A few months later I was at that same spot with my new large drum. It has a very deep tone and I was drumming slowly and turning it so that the sound would reverberate through the woods. As I turned it in one direction, I heard a large crack! The drum was a little intense, so I put it on a fallen cedar and began playing my guitar. I thought of a new song idea, so I turned my recorder on. Just before I began to play there are two rock clacks that can clearly be heard on the recording. At the time the rock clacks didn't register for me. I was too concentrated on recording the new song idea.

As I was sitting there playing, I closed my eyes and could hear someone coming over the fallen cedar I was next to. I didn't open my eyes and kept playing, because I knew my sasquatch friends were there.

Then, when it came time to leave, I picked the drum up that I had placed on the fallen cedar tree. I checked for the drumstick that I always put inside the drum, to make sure it was secure for the hike back. It was gone! I thought it might have dropped out of the drum while placing it on the fallen cedar? I turned on my flashlight and did a thorough search, but still didn't find it? I thought maybe I just couldn't see it in the dark? So, I went back early the next morning, as soon as it got light out and did another search. It was still gone! The picture below is of my great niece Ashlyn on that fallen cedar.

At the time, I thought C.C. had taken my drumstick. Now, I believe the young one I call Alice was the culprit. I decided that if she wanted the drumstick, she should have the drumstick. I now have another drumstick.

In August of 2017 there was a total eclipse that cut its way across the northern U.S. I planned to find a spot within the shadow of the totality where I could watch it in its full splendor. It would be the second total eclipse I've experienced during my life. The first time I was living in Bay Center, Washington and it was cloudy. With overcast skies during the eclipse, that experience was somewhat of a ho hum. I was determined not to let that happen again, so I planned to go east of the cascades to insure a good view. I decided to go to the Umatilla National Forest in northeast Oregon. My cousin Sam was living in Richland Washington at the time, I called and asked if he'd like to come along? He did and it was a nice quick trip. My cousin Sam plays the keyboards. He informed me ahead of time to bring my guitar and an amplifier for a jam with his friends. We had a fun night playing before leaving the next morning for the location I'd picked out.

The next day we made our way to an isolated camp site. Those mountains were full of eclipse enthusiasts, but we lucked out and found the perfect, isolated spot. Early on the morning of the eclipse I had rolled out of my tent and was pretty sure I heard some sasquatch calling from a distance. It always lifts my spirits to hear them.

I left my flip flops next to the car and put my heavy hiking boots on for hiking up to the rocky ridge above us. The eclipse was arriving at 10:30 in the morning at that location. The plan was to rush down the hill after the event and quickly change out my boots for the flip flops for what would be a long, hot drive back home. I thought we might beat most of the traffic, if we were quick enough. The sky was clear as a bell. We could see smoke from a forest fire to the south that was slowly heading our way, but the eclipse beat it. The eclipse was a phenomenal experience. Something that I will always cherish. After the eclipse we rushed down to the Subaru and my flip flops were gone. I spent a few minutes looking for them before giving up. That few minutes put us in all the traffic that was heading back home after that great event. Were my flip flops taken by a sasquatch? I honestly don't know? But, if they wanted my flip flops, they were welcome to them.

Sam came back with me to my house for a few days. The drive back to Raymond took ten hours and we were exhausted. As we checked the pictures from that eventful day, I saw something in one of them that didn't look right? After zooming in on the object in the sky I realized that we had visitors that day. One picture had a violet and white disk-shaped craft, that was obviously cloaked while we were watching the eclipse.

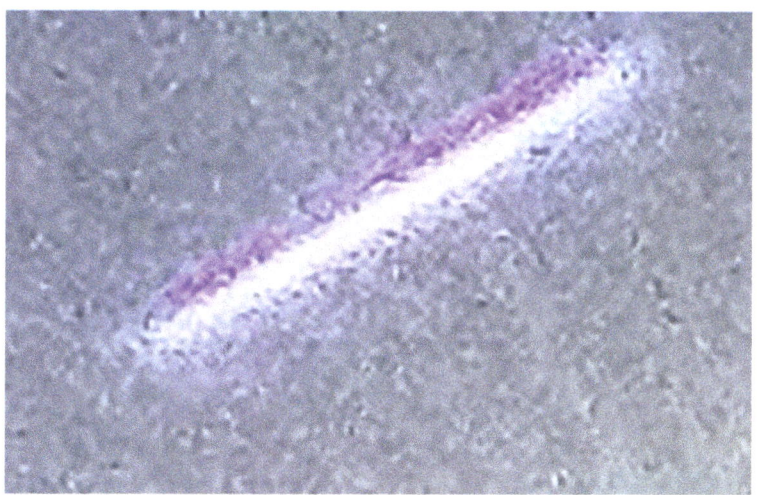

We sat around and had a conversation about the day and the UFO for just a few minutes before going to bed. Early the next morning we ate breakfast and headed out to camp in the Olympics. My plan was to introduce Sam to my sasquatch friends up there. I have many forest friends much closer to my house, but Sam had never camped in the Olympics and he was looking forward to seeing that gorgeous country. Besides, my friends up there can sing like no other sasquatch I've heard. Yes, they are artists and I'm a fan.

We camped near the Skykomish river. I now try and pick a spot not too close to a river or creek, so that the sound of rapids won't drown out the calls of my friends. I told Sam ahead of time that he would know when he heard them. That night Jacque, Peter, C.C and Alice came. They serenaded us with fervor. As soon as they began to call, Sam declared through his tent wall that I was right about knowing them when he heard them.

All three of the males called and blended their voices in the usual, but very unusual and beautiful way. I love their melodies. They are strong and primal, yet so gorgeous and exciting. Most of the time, they like to imitate owls. Thus, the insider joke "I heard some eight hundred-pound owls last night." My great friends up north also utilize elk and crow and other animal sounds for the blending of voices. They are my favorite trio. It is such an immersive and loving feeling they can project when singing. I will never get weary of hearing them.

Fortunately, they have gifted me the right to record their voices. In fact, the first night I turned my recorder on after almost two years, I had second thoughts. I went back to where I had mounted the recorder and attempted to turn it off. It wouldn't turn off. I pushed every button on the recorder and it wouldn't go off. Then, immediately after my attempt, they began to vocalize. I was so happy to know they had no problem with my recording their vocals. That particular recording has too much noise from the rapids. That is why I seek quieter locations where I can hear every detail of their voices. The next morning all the buttons worked again on the recorder and I was not surprised, I expect as much.

In June of 2020 I went camping in the local hills around my hometown. I brought my recorder and sent them a message that I was going to turn it on that night. I turned it on, but the device would only go to hold and none of the buttons worked. My thought at that time was that they might have something big planned and didn't want it recorded? It turned out they didn't come that night, as far as I know? I believe they were attempting to tell me that they knew I was out there and weren't coming, so they saved my batteries for me. Also, my labor, because I have to download the recording onto my computer and then utilize a program for isolating the vocals. So, they saved me at least a couple hours of labor as well.

Later at night, on that camp with Sam, I could hear some brush behind my tent rustling a bit. I heard someone come right up to my tent. The next morning, I found two prints. One up a path leading away from our tents and another one behind my tent. I'm sure they were made by Alice. They were about the size of a young preteen girl. I'm willing to bet they are bigger than mine by now.

I had found Alice's prints before. That time I was camping at another location inside the Olympic Park itself. I woke up early, before it was light out and I heard them playing across the river. I went over there and checked the area for prints and found one set that was the size of a five-year-old. I could tell she was running on all fours and yes, I already had the impression that it was a girl. I saw one perfect right foot print and then I could see where she had put her hand on a log, then beyond the log was the left foot print. It was obvious she had been moving very fast because of the length of the stride. I was amazed that a small being could actually move like that!

In the early summer of 2018, I was standing outside my tent, up in the Olympics, when I heard what sounded like a ten-year-old girl scream at me. I believe she wanted recognition. That's when I named her Alice, because she is in wonderland. She screamed from the same location Peter had screamed from, five years before. That made me chuckle when I thought about it. I'm thinking she did that on purpose to amuse me and say, "Hey, I'm here too!!!" Just as her brother had said, "Hey, I'm here!!!". A joke five years in the making.

I was glad that I could give my cousin Sam such a terrific experience. He wants to go again, of course.

The last campout of that season I was alone. I had stayed in an Olympic National Park campground that was almost empty by that time of year. They came early in the morning and were just outside the campground when they began to vocalize. I was so excited that I threw my clothes on in haste. I sent them a message that I was coming and ran out into the woods to them. I heard one call, that I suspect was Peter. He was very close and I began to walk in that direction when I heard Jacque call from behind me. I was directly between the two. I began calling back, because I was so happy! We were all happy! Dawn was just beginning to make it light out and they had to go.

As I was walking back into camp there was a confused looking man outside his tent, so I asked him if he had heard anything? "Yes, I thought if I unzipped my door and looked outside, I would have seen them walk by!!" was his exact reply. I find it interesting that they were imitating owls and yet this man, who had never heard a sasquatch call before, suspected that he was hearing sasquatch. Like I say, once you've heard them, you'll know, or you should know?

We chatted for some time and I found him a very interesting person. It turned out that he was newly retired and lived right on the northern edge of the Olympics on a property with some apple trees. I assumed his orchard was being visited during harvest time.

He mentioned that a very strange occurrence years before in the San Benito mountains made him think he might have already had an encounter with a sasquatch. He told me that he was a therapist and twice during his long career he had shared dreams with his clients. One of those times husband, wife and he all had the same exact dream on the same night. So, he was definitely a believer in telepathy. I liked him, so I asked if he'd like to get to know the forest people? He did not hesitate in answering "Yes!". So, I gave him some tips on how to begin an interaction by leaving gifts in his orchard, placing his hands on a tree and telling them, telepathically, that he would like to know them. I wonder how that went?

When I go out, I try and always stop and place my hands on a tree to send some good energy into it. I imagine my energy flowing up to the top and down into the roots and then out to the rest of nature. I then pray and thank the creator and all who are involved for everything they've taught me and for my fantastic, mysterious and fun filled life. I send my love to all of the creatures in nature, Gaia, the universe and especially my sasquatch friends. Then I ceremoniously kiss the tree.

One time, I was camping near Wynootchee lake when they came. There was a loud, young people party going on a few hundred yards away. I could hear the revelers easily because of the still night. Other than the partiers, I first heard a spotted owl call, which sounded much wimpier than my forest friends. When my friends began to call to me, the party participants began to laugh and even attempted to imitate the call. Then when C.C arrived and my forest friends jumped the volume up a bunch, the party died. I never heard them again that night. I would assume they became somewhat concerned as to what it was, they were actually hearing? Again, they were imitating owls and yet I could tell the glampers knew they were hearing something unusual.

Speaking of assumptions, you might notice that I make a few? I assume, because I believe, I know what I know. I would liken it to tracking. I have spent thousands of hours looking at tracks, of all kinds. It is something that happens, if you spend a lot of time out there. By the way, I've spent thousands of days and hundreds of nights in the wilderness. Much of that time I was on solo expeditions. I pay attention to my environment and everyone who is out there should do the same. When I find a track, I look for more. I also make conjectures about what they mean? That is what a tracker does. If I come upon an elk track that shows it was running in a panic with fur flying off, I assume that elk had something on its back. There are no cougar tracks to be seen, but then the cougar is on the elks back, isn't it? I also know that there is no other predator out there that could cause such a scene. So, I assume that it was a cougar riding that elk. A sasquatch riding an elk would not make the fur fly. They would just break the elk's neck.

When you are in the wilderness you are constantly making assessments and sometimes those assessments lead to conjectures and assumptions. The more experience you have, the more precise your conjectures and assumptions will become, if you've paid attention? Will it begin to rain soon? Am I safe without my bear mace? Do these prints show the animal was nervous? Will it freeze tonight? What is that smell? A bear? Coyote? Elk? Deer? What made that sound?

A constant process of discovery and assessment takes place on a tour of the wilderness. If you aren't a fool, you begin to piece things together. "These elk were huddling together in this small open space and are shuffling around as if frightened, by what?" "I'm smelling strong urine from a bear who knows I'm here and wants me to know he's here. Oops, there's a sow with a cub around somewhere? Time to be careful." So, on and so forth.

In July, 2019, I picked up my great nephew Mason at his Muumuu's house and we went camping. I had a nice campsite picked out and we had a pleasant time setting up camp and chatting for a while. I then played my guitar for a bit. I got busy again setting up my hammock when I heard a weird noise and then some talking from the woods across the access road. Mason jumped up and declared "I hear talking in the woods!" I replied that I heard it too. After they were purposely detected, they went around the perimeter of our campsite, beyond where we could see them and played while mostly imitating crows. It was so much fun to hear them and sometimes they were moving very fast. Across the road we could hear a metallic knock once in a while, emanating from the woods. I assumed that was the adult. They left before it got dark, perhaps because there would be no moon that night? After we got into our beds, we heard the adult call back one last time from about a mile away and up the hill from us. It was a very bizarre vocal that was a mix of primate and owl. It began by winding up with a crescendo of both pitch and volume. It did give me a slight chill. I liked it.

From our campsite, they had headed south, so I assumed that was a hint to where they were living? The Becho clan had lived over that way and so we moved our camp up to that landing for the next night. I believe that is all state forest now and the gate is now open. Unfortunately, the Becho family doesn't live there anymore. I camped, alone up there in the spring of 2019 and had left a glyph of an ex made out of two sticks. When Mason and I returned to camp there in July they had changed the glyph to a symbol that looks like a lower-case h, or chair, by breaking one of the sticks in half.

I did find that in old Spanish Iberic, it might mean protector or signs?

When I was there alone in the spring, two males came and vocalized to me just after I got into my car for bedtime. I had forgotten my tent. I jumped out of the sleeping bag as quickly as possible and went to where I knew they could see me. They were down the road a few hundred yards with a direct view of me. It was too dark for me to see them. After they both called to me, utilizing the owl vocal, I called back attempting to match their skill. It was the best I'd ever done and they got quiet all of a sudden. In my mind's eye I saw them looking at each other in surprise and giving a nod of approval. Then they took off in two different directions and called until their voices faded away. One went west and the other went south. I knew they were showing me that they weren't located at the Becho site anymore and if I wanted to find them, I'd have to go west or south. I believe the one that went west might have been my teacher? The one that went south was the one that called back to Mason and I the day of our visit from the juveniles.

After they left, I turned on my recorder. I really didn't even think they would return, so I didn't check that recording for about a year. It turns out they had returned and vocalized again later that night. Unfortunately, I was sleeping in my car and did not wake up to hear them.

Near the end of our adventure my nephew and I were discussing my lifestyle and we both agreed that I was the luckiest man in the world! Okay, I might have prompted his support for my assessment a little? It is the way I feel, though.

Our final night, we spent on my back deck, looking at the stars. Mason has had a keen interest in astronomy for a few years now and lives in southern California, so, he was excited to see the stars so clearly. You can't see the milky way down in southern California if you are on the coast. We spotted the international space station fly over and then a couple of white flashing lights hovering straight above us at high altitude kept us company. The picture below was taken from my back deck.

Russell Wiitala

CHAPTER 8

Montana House of Mystery

As I HAVE explored the esoteric realms of metaphysics and sasquatch I've gone to a few gatherings or summits for UFOs and bigfoot and met some very nice people. They are intelligent and very earnest in their pursuit for the truth. The ones I call my friends are a subset of sasquatch researchers. They are the woo knowers, like me. We all have had extraordinary experiences with sasquatch and most of us with spirits, ET's and or UFOs, as well.

Every once in a while, we manage to get together and exchange notes and ideas, usually at a summit. It is always very entertaining and informative to hear someone else's encounters and experiences.

I met my friend, Joe Hauser, at a sasquatch summit in Ocean Shores Washington. I learned that he owned the Montana Vortex and House of Mystery, in Columbia Falls, Montana. Joe had bought it to study it. I suddenly felt a compulsion to visit at the earliest opportunity.

Joe is a wildlife expert by training. He said, while out in the field, sasquatch had been tapping him on the shoulder for years before he acknowledged them. He told me he finally came to the conclusion that they were real and asked, "Okay, you're real, now what?"

I believe the, "now what?", was Joe buying the vortex. Just as I felt compelled to visit Joe and his wife Tammy at the vortex, I'm thinking he was compelled to buy it. I'm making an assumption here based on what I know. Joe may totally disagree with me? I do know they have the ability to guide us. We do have choice. I am sure I've done more than a couple of things differently, than they would have wanted. They also cater to what we want to know. Did our pre-mission questionnaire reveal what we were curious about as part of the vetting process? I'm being a little facetious, but somehow, they picked us for a reason?

The day I found the meteorite did they know where I was going and where I would be standing when I found it? Perhaps they can look into the future and see where I was going to stand or perhaps, they guided me to stand there? I believe it has to be one of these options. There is a wild possibility that it was a coincidence? I highly doubt that.

When David Crockett first went to Texas, he had an encounter with what I can only surmise was a sasquatch. He had telepathic communication with a huge, hairy, naked man and was warned by him that he should not come back to Texas. Of course, he did and lost his life at the Alamo. That incident, recorded in his journal, makes me believe they possess the ability of precognition. In other words, they can see into the future.

A few weeks before my trip to Montana I was out hiking the same log road where the crystal was left for me. I hiked up to a point where I could look down a beautiful valley with Smith creek running through it. As I was standing there, I heard a tree go down on another ridge. I knew my teacher wanted me to go over there. It was too far to hike that day, so I went the next day.

For the weeks leading up to hiking up to that ridge, I had been thinking that I would like to see a print again, since it had been a while. As I hiked up to the ridge, I found a track line with three prints in semi-frozen alder leaves. That made me happy, because it was the first time, I'd seen my teachers prints. They appeared to measure around sixteen or seventeen inches. That night the rain came and the prints were gone. I'm pretty sure my teacher was aware that would happen. I took a picture of the best one and continued up the road to the ridge.

I hiked around and tried to find what he had in store for me? After a few trips up there, I finally came upon a mature noble fir with a very strange pattern carved on it. It appeared as if someone had used a small hatchet and had taken off 3 inches by 3-inch squares of bark off the tree. The pattern was about five squares wide and six squares down. Underneath the pattern were two gouges that looked as if they were made with an elk horn. The pattern was eye level to me and about fifteen feet off of the ground, as it was located down a steep slope off the road I was on.

I took a picture of it and was anxious to see what Joe might have to say about it? A few days before leaving for Montana I checked my camera for the picture. It was gone? There were a few days before I was leaving, so I decided to hike back up there and take another picture. When I got to the location where I took the picture, the tree was gone! As if it had never existed. In fact, there were at least three other trees missing that had been nearby.

After thinking about it I decided it must have been a lesson in the Mandela effect. The Mandela effect is when you have slipped into an alternative, parallel universe. In this case I believe the tree was slipped into a parallel universe, while I remained in this universe where the tree never existed. I also assumed there must be a demarcation line or ley line where the trees were.

Awhile later, I was hiking down from that ridge when I heard a very loud jet engine. It was very abrupt and loud for about five seconds and then cut off and went completely silent. There was not a cloud in the sky and there was no jet to be seen? Then, after about fifteen seconds of dead silence, it did the same thing again and was done. The engine cut off and on like someone flipped a switch on a PA system. I'm thinking my teacher was manipulating that demarcation line or ley line? Could it have been a sound that was crossing the line of metaphysical power from another parallel universe?

It is amazing how my perceptions and interpretations have changed over these last few years. When I first began to write this book, I hadn't experienced any of this. I started writing this book five years ago, but my devotion to it has been sporadic. I'm glad it was, because so much more has happened during the interim.

Before personally experiencing any metaphysics connected with sasquatch, I had heard some stories that I thought sounded a bit too fantastical. Yet I could detect the sincerity of those who related their stories to me. I'm glad now I did not dismiss them outright. I kept an open mind. How could I know what they had experienced? I was not there.

Now, I don't question too much, because when I do, I often miss something fantastic. Now, when strange occurrences take place, I wonder how they relate to what I'm experiencing with sasquatch and ET? I usually don't immediately search for a, so called, rational explanation. It's much quicker to cut to the chase. It's like the assumptions I make when I see a print that looks like an elk made it. Without hesitation I figure an elk made that print. When I hear human like voices out in the woods, I figure forest people are talking to each other and not homo sapien sapiens. That attitude comes from accumulated experience. Sometimes I'm surprised and it turns out I was wrong. I just make the safest bet on what I know and have experienced.

I made it a quick, three-day trip to Columbia Falls, Montana in June of 2018. I drove all day and camped just a couple hours' drive from The House of Mystery, in Lolo National Forest. That night I didn't receive a visit from the local sasquatch population. That is actually unusual for me. I kind of expected one, but there was a very hard, cold rain that night. The next morning the sun came out in all of its glory. I was able to dry out my tent quickly, break camp and get on the road.

Joe and Tammy were busy giving tours when I arrived, so I joined Joe's tour. On the tour I took some pictures inside the house of mystery. In a couple of them the windows are displaced and orbs can be seen. Also, big spaces between the boards of the walls were brightly lit up. The boards don't have large spaces between them. In the picture below you can see how bright the window is and below it, slightly to the right, you can see green foliage in a displaced phantom window. To the left of the phantom window you can see an orb and below the orb is a possible mist, of some sort? To me, the brightness between the boards and out the window hints at a dielectric power.

Quite often photos taken within the vortex and especially within the walls of the house of mystery show strange and unusual phenomena. Sometimes it will be someone who wasn't present when the picture was taken and yet photo bombs the picture. Some pictures of people end up with displaced arms and legs. One picture I saw looked like a small sasquatch with a group of tourists.

After the tour, I spent the rest of the day wondering around and soaking up the ambiance of that sacred and powerful place. The local

Blackfoot tribe called it the place of no return. So, obviously, they knew something was up with it.

Joe and Tammy really keep it looking cute with all of the décor of masks attached to trees, park benches, brick designs, garden gnomes and so on. It is a peaceful, beautiful and harmonic place.

The vortex field reacts differently with different people. It has a personality and will shut down when certain people are there. Joe told me that some people are driven away. On more than one occasion a person has paid for the tour, moved to the orientation box at the beginning of the tour, then turned around and gone back to their car and left without explanation or asking for a refund. It can also become quite animated with certain other visitors. The powers of the vortex fields vary from day to day and even moment to moment. Some of that depends on the energy humans bring to it.

Joe also told me that three times over the years, young "Indigos" (sensitive children) have mentioned the Viking guard standing between two trees near the entrance to the tour? All three described him the same, huge, blond hair with beard in full armor. Could that be why some tourists have left? Could the guard be sending them a telepathic message to leave? I gazed in the direction of the guard and gave him deference, while politely asking permission to enter. He did not drive me away.

The tour was very fun and educational. Joe did an excellent job with all of the demonstrations. There is a wooden board that demonstrates how people get smaller as they go from one end to the other. Two people stand on the board and then switch ends. Anyone can see that the people change size from one end of the board to the other. It is not an optical illusion. Sometimes people can appear to change height by as much as six inches. There is a level that can be used by any suspicious participants, to show that the board is on flat, level ground.

In the House of Mystery there is also, what I believe, is a heavy piece of logging gear hanging down that will swing easily in one direction, but not in the other? Also, a broom can easily be stood on end in that weird building, with very little effort.

During a break, Joe drove me up to a reservoir that is nearby. On the way back down, I spotted a very fresh break of a four-inch-thick tree, right next to the road. I believe it happened while we were up at the dam. I thanked the tree breaker in my head and told Joe I consider that an invitation.

After they closed for the day, Joe had to go change a propane tank on Nick Nelson's trailer. I stayed in the house and conversed with Tammy. While we were talking, we heard the sliding glass door open and shut. The sliding glass door is just around the corner and could not be seen from where we were seated. Tammy looked at me and said "Joe is changing the propane tank." I jumped up and rushed to the door, but nothing was there. I stepped out onto the deck and looked around but saw nothing. That really got me excited and looking forward to going out that night with Joe. I considered that a teaser for what was to come.

Going out at night with joe was an amazing experience! We saw unattached shadows paralleling our movements. We saw white and red orbs up on top of the mountain across the highway. We heard a sasquatch scream from across the highway. At one-point Joe told me "They" wanted me to go into what is called the labyrinth, which is in the eye of the vortex they call Khafre. As I was standing in the middle of the labyrinth, I felt the presence of entities around and above me. I looked up and thanked them for being there for me. I experienced a profound feeling of love and belonging within the labyrinth. Joe took a couple of pictures before his battery went dead. He told me that premature death of a battery is a frequent occurrence at the vortex. The pictures showed orbs, a dark floating shadow that looked like the shadow of a manta ray and some white ectoplasmic mist floating above me. Unfortunately, Joe can't find those pictures.

At one point we were in the house of mystery looking out the window and talking when we heard an exhale of breath from something big, not too far behind us. In fact, I interpreted it as a cloaked sasquatch. That is probably who opened and closed the sliding door, too?

At the end of the night, we said goodnight and I went into the public restroom as Joe went into the house. As I was standing over the urinal the door opened and shut, by itself. I said hello, but there was no response. I'm not sure if he was coming in or going out?

I put an audio recorder out overnight and got a lot of shuffling sounds and doors opening and closing, but the traffic from the highway was so noisy and disruptive I deleted it. All in all, it was an amazing experience. Joe even let me pitch my tent in the vortex itself. Unfortunately, I was so tired I fell right to sleep and experienced nothing but a deep slumber. The next morning, after I left, Joe found a glyph near where I left the recorder. It was made of a stick with two sticks crossing it.

A lot of strange things happen at the vortex. Sasquatch is seen, on average, about three times a season in broad daylight by tourists there. Joe says he'll be working in the gift shop when a tourist comes running in, all excited, telling him a bigfoot just ran through the vortex. By the time Joe gets out there, it's gone. In 2019, Joe finally saw one disappear in front of his eyes after he was informed there was one in the vortex and went to check.

Joe has owned the vortex for over fifteen years as of this writing. So that means, if you extrapolate the numbers, sasquatch has made over forty appearances on the property during that time, in broad daylight. They finally put security cameras out in the fall of 2019. Within the house of mystery, a huge being in the shape of a sasquatch was recorded glowing with white energy. The silhouette was well defined, with a conical head on top of huge, muscular shoulders. Then he morphed into an ectoplasmic mist and floated up and out of camera view. Joe saw him on the monitor located in their house and quickly went to check the house of mystery. In the recording Joe can be seen not glowing bright, like the figure that was just there a few moments before. Joe is a stocky six-footer and it was also apparent that the glowing being was much more massive than Joe.

As I left for home Joe gave me a book, The Golden Vortex by Nick Nelson and a pamphlet entitled Two- One -Six, also authored by Nick. I only talked with Nick briefly while I was there. Joe and I told him about our adventures the night before and Nick told me about some of the things he'd witnessed there at the vortex. He said he saw a thunderbird fly over one day. It appeared over the vortex and then disappeared when it exited the other end. When I saw the title of the pamphlet, Two-One-Six, I knew, immediately, the number I was given over and over through the years had to do with vortex fields.

327 is a number that has shown up over and over in my life through the years. It showed up so often that I took notice. I considered it my number, but I didn't know why? The last time I saw it I was checking into the Quinault Casino hotel. I had shown up for the sasquatch summit

and went to the desk in case there were any cancellations? The young lady at the desk was just hanging up the phone and informed me the call happened to be a cancellation. She checked me into the only vacancy there was in the hotel, room 327.

When I learned of my room number, I got a huge chill. I knew it was not a coincidence. How did they arrange that? Somehow, they had created a situation for the people who had the reservation for that room? A situation serious enough for them to cancel their reservation. I would love to know what that was? Perhaps two flat tires, or maybe just a change of the mind? It would not be the last time such an arrangement seemed to be made for me. Perhaps, "they" were the ones who made the reservation in the first place?

After that, the number disappeared for a few years. When Joe handed me the Two-One-Six pamphlet upon my departure, I immediately realized that if you add one digit to each number of 216, you get 327. I then understood 327 had something to do with the Montana vortex. Or, perhaps, vortex fields in general?

The number 327 hasn't flashed in front of my face for a few years now. The number has changed to 111 since my trip to the Montana vortexes. 327-216=111. Now I believe it is about 111 and 327 was just a means to an end. They may have picked 327 because 111 is a much more common number merely by being lower. I love baseball, for instance and I can see 111 pop up during almost any game, at least once or twice. They picked 327 because it was less common, so that I would notice it. I usually see 111 several times a day now.

I did find that 216 doubled is 432. 432 -327 = 105. 111 divided by 105=1.0(571428)...which, beyond the decimal point and the first 0, is a repeating sequence of numbers usually created by dividing a number by 7. For instance, 360 divided by 7=51.428(571428)...putting the repeating sequences in parenthesis. Dividing any number by 7 other than a multiple of 7 will produce this same reciprocating set of numbers. The first digit beyond the decimal point begins the sequence and can be any one of the six digits in the sequence. Then it repeats for eternity.

What might be the significance of 7? 360 divided by 7 also produces the angle of the slope on the face of the great pyramid when rounded off, which is 51.4 degrees.

The Greeks referred to pi as 3 and 1/7th. If you divide 327 by 216 you get 1.5138888888... Ignore the 1 to the left of the decimal point, then move the decimal point two positions to the right and you get 51.4 again, when rounded off. So, maybe it really is about 327? I do know 327 is a strange number. Also, notice the repeating sequence is missing 3,6 and 9. Tesla said that if you understand 3, 6 and 9, you understand the universe. Maybe the six-digit sequence represents the other side of the veil? Perhaps Nichola Tesla could have said "If you understand 3,6 and 9, you will understand the visible, 3D universe?

This is what I do with the limited information I receive. It is like a labyrinth. I keep trying passageways and most end in a dead end, but sooner or later, I make some progress.

Who are these beings, beside sasquatch, that are guiding me to this information? I can't say for sure. I believe it is ET, or possibly elementals and or spirits of some kind? When Russell Wilson and I went to the UFO summit in February of 2019, I expected to get a familiar number at the motel check-in, we got room 111.

On our way to the summit, Russell and I went to a couple valleys up in the Olympics that we had never been to. The first one was very beautiful and it wasn't long before we heard a tree limb crack. Then we drove to the next valley and ended up at an out of season campground. We heard three knocks very soon after arrival. I said to Russell "Hey, what's up with that? We're friends and family, we should be hearing one knock." Soon after, one knock was heard. We both got a good laugh out that. I have come to the conclusion, after reading and talking to many witnesses, three knocks mean human and one means friend or family.

The next week Russell went to Astoria and checked into the last room they had available at that motel, room 111. This number still haunts me. I obviously haven't figured it out yet and they obviously want me to. I'm sure, like the internet tells me, it's not about angel 111. It is about vortex fields and possibly portals?

What is a vortex? A tornado, hurricane, or the water going down a drain in a sink all create a spinning vortex. In the case of the Montana vortex, it is a field spinning, counterclockwise, around a central point. like a sea shell, pine cone or hurricane the pattern of demarcation lines from an electromagnetic vortex spirals out in a Fibonacci sequence. The vortex acts as if it's magnetic and yet a magnet does not react to it?

In the 12th century Leonardo Fibonacci took the number 1 and doubled it. Then he took that sum of 2 and added the previous number 1 equaling 3. To continue he then added 3 to the previous sum of 2 equaling 5. Then he took 5 and added the previous sum of 3 which results in 8 and so on. The Fibonacci sequence begins with numbers 1,1, 2, 3, 5, 8, 13, 21, 34, 55, 89, with the 12th iteration being 144. It also can be described as a progression at a ratio of 1.618. All of nature follows this pattern, one way or the other.

When I look at an ancient Sumerian carving that represents a god with a pine cone in his extended hand, it makes me wonder? The pine cone spirals outward from the center where the seed is cradled, in the eye. A symbolic seed of life? I see that pine cone as symbolic of that god's gift of knowledge. The key to understanding the basic fundamentals of our universe.

The vortex varies in strength or amplitude from day to day. Some of this is by schedule, so Nick Nelson discovered. Other reasons are more mysterious?

Physicists will tell you that an electron has to spin 720 degrees to complete a 360-degree round trip back to its original position. The electron is not only moving in a figure eight, like the fields of a magnet, but it is also doing barrel rolls as it does it. If you take a strip of paper, then tape the two ends together, twist it one revolution into a mobius strip, it will replicate the figure eight route of an electron. Once around its spin is down and then on the second time around it has come back to be in its original upright position for the completion of one, 360-degree revolution. In the meantime, it's been there, here, there and back again. Where is there?

Before going any further, I want to explain the measurements of distance and their resulting ratios and sums don't add up when the metric system is applied to any of this. Instead, everything works with inches, cubits and miles. This really threw me at first and then I learned that these units of measurement are ancient and go way back before recorded history.

Nobody knows where modern metrology came from? Also, the same numbers 3, 6, 9, 12, 36, 60, 72, 108, 216, 360, 432, 864 show up in ancient cultures all across the earth.

The Babylonian's long unit of measure, the kashu, was 129,600 susi in length which is 360 squared. Maneh was a unit for measuring volume and was 7776 cubic modern inches, but 21,600 um, to them. The Roman load was 3,000 libra or 2,160 pounds today. The Egyptian cubit is 25 pyramid inches. Otherwise known as the sacred biblical cubit. The earth's polar axis is 400,000 cubits long.

What about the metric system? It was invented by the French in relatively recent times. The metric system does make an appearance in one instance, that I know of. The great pyramid lies on latitude 29.9792". Did you know the speed of light is 299,792,458 meters per second? What are the odds of those two numbers having the same order of sequence to the sixth digit by chance? Round off the speed of light to the nearest thousand and the two numbers are identical.

Could it be that we have forgotten about our visitors from the stars? Absence makes the heart grow fonder, unless of course you are an extra-terrestrial that gifts mankind advanced mathematical concepts and astronomical knowledge.

Within the center of the vortex field there is an eye that is quiet. Bordering that eye is the first demarcation line. Demarcation lines are where anomalies take place. Think of a demarcation line as an apex of a wave. Like waves moving out from the center of a pebble being thrown into a pond, they move away from the center.

What is happening at the boards where guests switch positions and change size? I believe the Montana vortex fields are magnets on end. The flow going in a counterclockwise direction would indicate that the magnet is sticking with its negative, or north pole above ground. That would mean that the inertial plane, or center of the magnet between the poles, sits beneath the ground. The following link is to a video by Ken Wheeler that illustrates the structure of a magnet. https://youtu.be/5Gbng1wm62M

I believe space itself it getting squeezed at a demarcation line. Time slows within the vortex field. A watch will lose two seconds a day within the Montana vortex, compared to an identical watch outside of the vortex. Two seconds a day is significant. Physicists will tell you that time is affected by gravity and gravity is affected by mass. The closer to a large mass you roam, the slower time runs relative to where there is less mass. According to Ken Wheeler, mass is caused by magnetism.

Ken Wheeler, A.K.A. Theoria Apophasis, discovered the grand unifying theory, 1/Phi cubed, which calculates to 4.23606. He came up with it after studying Pythagorean's secret theorem. Ken teaches that magnetism has different states like water. Water can be solid, liquid or gas. Magnetism can be gravity, electric or magnetic. All three states from the same thing.

A magnet has a coherent set of atoms that are polarized. In other words, all, or most of the magnetic fields of the atoms are aligned in the same direction. Earth does not have this coherency as the atoms are not polarized and random in their configuration. Gravity is weak magnetism caused by incoherency of all the poles of its atoms pointing in random directions in any given body. Yes, I'm telling you that your body is incoherent, as far as magnetism is concerned.

With a magnet, the greater the force, the smaller the magnetic field. So, is the power of the Montana vortex creating a compact and powerful field? I would say yes and its power varies from day to day. When the two ends of the wood plank at the Montana vortex produce the greatest difference between one end and the other, its magnetism is the strongest. When it doesn't produce a great variance, then the magnet is weak. Why it varies might be due to the shifting of the iron nickel interior of the earth's interior? That is my wild guess.

I wrote that sentence above about my wild guess and then, soon after, I read scientists are talking about the shift in our magnetic pole possibly being caused by movement of huge iron nickel blobs deep in the interior of the earth. I'm willing to bet that is what effects the varying strength of the Montana vortex.

Upon arrival back home I had some reading to do. I found Nick Nelson's book, The Golden Vortex, fascinating. He grew up with an acute interest in magnetism. Blessed with a sharp mind and an unrelenting obsession, he has learned a lot about both magnets and vortex fields over several decades. Nick has worked for years at both the Oregon vortex and the Montana vortex in an effort to try and figure them out. He was the one who noticed that the placement of commercial vortices in the western U.S. mirrored, from the belt down, the constellation Orion, when viewed on a map. The Oregon vortex and the two commercial ones in California are in the configuration of Orion's belt. With the bottom two stars in the constellation represented by the Montana House of Mystery and another commercial vortex in South Dakota. Those vortex fields were discovered and individually turned into commercial enterprises over a period of decades. There was no collaboration of where to put them. The vortex fields were already there and humans detected them and then exploited them by turning them into a commercial enterprise. So how did they come to be in the configuration of Orion?

Nick also figured out that both the external and internal structures of the great pyramid are laid out on the grounds of the Oregon vortex.

Through attempts at ground surveying, he discovered that the ground itself warps, unnoticeably to witnesses, with a six-degree oscillation. It is impossible within the vortex to utilize survey instruments to accurately plot the land. The readings from those instruments will change from minute to minute.

Soon after reading his book, I was on the road to visit some friends, Tobe Johnson and Eryn Jackson. Tobe was conducting a pod cast called Strange Brau at the Axe and the Fiddle in Cottage Grove, Oregon. I participated as a live audience member and even told one or two of my favorite sasquatch stories on air.

After the podcast I took off for Florence Oregon. I did not have any kind of map app at the time and the signage was lacking. So, I decided to do it the old-fashioned way with a fold up map. It was not useful; the roads were not on the map. There was plenty of sun left to drive to the coast and set up camp. So, I essentially pointed my trusty Subaru to the west and used the sun as a guide while driving the back-country roads. There was very light traffic. I might have seen three vehicles in the first forty-five minutes of driving.

The scenery was gorgeous. Everything was lush and green, or in bloom. I enjoyed the drive very much and decided I must return there someday and camp out in that beautiful country.

After a while, I came around a bend and saw a yearling black bear crossing the road. It was close enough that I hit the brakes. There was a steep, barren incline, that he would have to negotiate. I was excited because I could stop the car and watch him climb the slope right next to me. At least, that was my thought.

As he ran across the highway, he took a leap towards the slope and disappeared! It was as if he jumped into an invisible door. I came to a halt right where I planned on watching him climb, but he was nowhere to be seen? Where did he go!? I sat there and looked at the barren slope. There was little debris or vegetation to hide behind. There was no cave or hole for him to jump into. The drainage ditch was about a foot deep and had very little vegetation, so, he certainly wasn't hiding in the ditch. I was stunned!

I sat there for five minutes and thought about what might have just happened? I finally had to come to the conclusion that I'd just seen a bear disappear without the aid of a magician. Or, at least, the kind of magician that works the Las Vegas strip.

When I got home, I decided to check a chart Nick Nelson had in his book of regional vortex fields. My bear disappearing episode happened on one of the demarcation lines for a regional vortex that has an eye between Klamath Falls and Gold Hill Oregon.

How did Nick Nelson plot those regional vortices? He used a map and a pendulum. In other words, he divined the location. He didn't know if it would work? Nick will express surprise at such an idea actually working and yet I know it worked.

Quite often, their lessons are layered. I had been thinking during the previous few days that it had been a while since I had seen a bear. Joe Hauser had posted a picture of a sow and a couple of cubs just a few days before on Facebook and it had me thinking of bears. I wanted to see a bear, so they showed me a bear and combined it with a lesson and message. The lesson was a demonstration on where there is metaphysical power. The message was to take Nick Nelson and his book seriously!

If I have to take his book seriously then I have to consider Nick a genius for coming up with all of what he discovered. He claims it was just one incremental step at a time and most of his acquired knowledge came through serendipity. I would say genius is persistence. Nick has been a very persistent soul when it comes to vortex fields and magnets. Also, when something serendipitous or unexpected happens to someone, that person then has to have the motivation and deductive ability to "figure it out.".

There is an incident that Nick relates in his book that took place on the same demarcation line where I saw a disappearing bear. Mine took place on the north, northwest part of that line and his took place on the south, southeast section of that same demarcation line. Mine took place in Oregon and his in California, 180 degrees from each other on the same demarcation line that forms a 360-degree circle. When I realized that, I was floored! That convinced me that his divining was very accurate.

Nick experienced his event in 1974, on the same demarcation line as my incident, except it was the part that runs through northern California. He and a friend were driving to Reno Nevada for a gambling trip. They had just filled their bellies at a restaurant and were back on the road when they instantly found themselves 100 miles down the highway. Nick, in his shock, pulled over to the side of the road. He asked his friend "What just happened?" His friend didn't know? They began to question each other about the previous few minutes? Both agreed they couldn't remember passing familiar landmarks? They both checked their watches and only about three minutes had passed since he had checked his watch, soon after leaving the restaurant. Also, they both were starving, as if they hadn't eaten in a couple of days, even though they had just eaten.

Jumping to conclusions again, I believe they know of Nick's book and they knew that I would check his charts. I knew why they did it there, but I did not know how? Obviously, they chose a very powerful demarcation line for that lesson. I also believe they might have subconsciously manipulated the divining pendulum Nick was using over the map. Or, could it be, that Nick's subconscious was tapping into what has been called the Akashic record? The Akashic record is a universal bank of knowledge that some say can be accessed through meditation.

These next few paragraphs are somewhat technical. I am attempting to explain magnetism in a very compact and cogent way. It is simplex and yet difficult to explain in simple terms. So, if you have difficulty don't worry about understanding every nuance, the pain will end soon.

Ken Wheeler explains mass as the result of magnetism. "Magnetism, denotatively, is a 3D dimensional S curve that extrapolates out a forced vector. Force by definition is centrifugal. Force by definition is expansive." Think of that curve as two interlocking corkscrews in a hour glass formation. Nothing exists within our 3D world without magnetism. He goes on to explain that there are only two forces at work in our universe. One is centrifugal divergence and the other is centripetal convergence, which ultimately forms a toroidal field as the vectors intertwine.

The field is accelerating into and out of the inertial plane or counter space that lies in the center between two poles of a magnet. Counter space means there is no space. In between the force vectors of magnetism is the dielectric field. Electricity is a hybrid of magnetism and the dielectric field.

The inertial plane is the source of all matter and energy. It is the counter space between two poles in a magnet. It is the depository from which all things come. You can think of the inertial plane as the puppet master who manipulates his puppets. The puppets are all made of the same cloth, which is magnetism. The main puppets in the play are dielectric, magnetism and electricity. When the magnetic field overcomes the inertial plane or ether, it can manifest into a dielectric condensate, otherwise known as mass.

Ken goes on to teach that everything in the universe is magnetic. Gravity itself is just a weak manifestation of magnetism between objects that lack field coherency. In other words, the north and south poles of every atom in earth are pointing in random directions. A magnet, on the other hand has all or most of the poles of its atoms polarized. The poles of its atoms are lined up in the same direction which creates field coherency. So, the field incoherency of all the earths atoms creates a weak magnetic effect we refer to as gravity.

A magnetic field grows smaller as the power of a magnet is increased. You can think of this in terms of wave length. The larger the wave length the lesser the power. For instance, the wave length of the visual spectrum is weak compared to a stronger more compact wave length, such as micro or gamma waves. With a strong enough dialectic field, you can shrink the mass of an object right out of the visible universe, like a black hole.

The vectors of the field of a magnet are in an hour glass, figure eight shape, with cones that form two vortex patterns corkscrewing, creating a toroidal or donut shape. Ken calls it a reciprocating, dielectric hyperbola. What is reciprocating is the magnetic field, with interlacing vectors spinning in opposite directions that appear to create the same pattern seen in a dream catcher. You will see the same dream catcher pattern manifest when a magnet is placed under a ferro cell. These vectors enter and exit the center of the magnet where counter space or the inertial plane is.

There are very high-definition pictures of the sun that show a pattern, scientists call a huge plasma storm. That storm is actually a gigantic magnet several times larger than the earth. It mirrors the same pattern produced by a magnet as seen under a ferro cell.

Counter space, or inertial plane is the route by which two electrons can be entangled to the extent that you can take one across the universe and they will communicate instantaneously regardless of the distance. Counter space means no space. Everything is connected to everything else through counter space, otherwise known as the inertial plane.

The inertial plane can be found between the north and south pole of a magnet. It lies at the intersection of the hour glass configuration the field of a magnet forms. When two magnets are combined, the fields combine to form one magnet. If you cut a magnet in half a kazillion times, it will still be a magnet with the inertial plane in the middle. Two magnets are not attracted to each other, they are attempting to dive into the inertial plane that lies between them.

What goes on throughout the universe is the constant motion of magnetic field mediation. All of these magnetic fields trying to find balance and the inertial plane adjusting accordingly within those fields. According to Ken Wheeler, time does not exist. Everything we perceive as time is created by magnetic field mediation.

Did they, somehow, utilize the dielectric power at that point of the demarcation line, causing a portal or worm hole to open up in which the bear disappeared? Is the demarcation line a vector for the field of a huge magnet, otherwise known as a vortex field?

I'm thinking portals must be connected through the inertial plane. There is no time or space in the inertial plane and therefore stepping into a portal will instantly transport you to another world, potentially thousands or millions of light years away. A being, or bear, could be accelerating into the inertial plane only to emerge out the other side through, a sort of central fugal divergence. The portal being the inertial plane that lies in between the poles of a magnet. Are the two ends of a portal equivalent to the north and south poles of a magnet with the inertial field in the middle?

Are things such as animals, or even viruses coming through portals on earth from elsewhere. Many people report seeing Pterosaurs in the southwest deserts. Perhaps there are portals that link to ancient worlds too?

The, apparent, sasquatch recorded in the House of Mystery was glowing very brightly with dielectric energy. That could explain how he became a disappearing mist. The dialectic would overcome the magnetic in his body and he would disappear from our visible world. I'm also sure the sasquatch knew he was on camera and was giving a demonstration of one of their powers. Within a few days Joe Hauser was showing that recording to a stunned audience at the Quinault Sasquatch Summit.

All of this made me consider something else? Was Nick Nelson chosen for his genius persistence way back before 1974? I have come to the conclusion that there are several of us who were chosen, each for different reasons and assignments. How did that happen? Who did the choosing? When did it happen? Also, why?

There have been some strange things people kept telling me over and over. I had never heard anyone tell me "You've been chosen" before my entanglement with sasquatch. Yet, until I accepted it, I kept hearing "You've been chosen" from even people I wouldn't expect to say such a thing. I'd tell them one of my stories and they would tell me that I was chosen. "What? I don't think so. If they chose me, they must have made a mistake" I would say with humor.

I decided to investigate shamanism. To my surprise, I learned that most shaman don't volunteer to be a shaman, but are "chosen". In fact, most shaman resist their destiny and have difficult lives until they finally accept their position as a shaman.

After resisting the idea for a couple of years, I decided to accept my destiny and not fight it. I don't consider myself a shaman though. I think of myself as nothing more than a student, or seeker of esoteric metaphysical knowledge.

CHAPTER 9

Synchronicities

THE MONTANA VORTEX is actually three overlapping vortex fields. If you look at them from above, their eyes form the same pattern as Orion's belt. If you look at the five commercial vortex fields in the western U.S., they form the same pattern as the five stars at the bottom of the Orion constellation.

Also, Nick Nelson discovered that the outward shape of the Great Pyramid and its internal structure are laid out on the grounds of the Oregon Vortex.

The Khafre vortex is 216 feet wide. Confusion hill, which assumes the same position on the west coast vortexes as the Khafre vortex in Orion's belt, is also 216 feet wide. Confusion hill lies 216 miles from Mystery Spot, another commercial vortex in California and 216 miles from the Oregon vortex. All of this and more, Nick Nelson discovered over the years. Reading his book and recognizing the significance of 216 has led me to other discoveries that I'm sure they wanted me to find.

In fact, 216 shows up in the strangest ways throughout our solar system. 6 times 6 times 6 equals 216. Six, six, six is not an evil number, it's an expression of nature. There are 360 degrees in a circle. 6 times 360=2,160. Always eliminate the zeroes to illuminate the message.

The earliest known volume of a bushel is 2,160 cubic inches. Did you know the moon is just a mile plus shy of 2,160 miles wide? Did it shrink a little over the eons? If you take 216 and multiply it by four you will get 864. Add three zeroes to the end of 864 and you will end up with the diameter of the sun at 864,000 miles. Did you know there are 864,000 seconds in a day?

Joseph Campbell, the famous mythologist came up with 1,656 years from Adam's creation to Noah's ark. I don't know how he came up with that? What I do know is that there are 864,000 weeks in 1,656 years. Also, the human heart beats around 86,400 beats a day. I believe much of mythology to be based on actual facts and occurrences in history or were created to illuminate knowledge.

That doesn't mean you take myths as fact, but they do have something to teach. I see much of myth as actual accounts that, through oral tradition, have been told and retold by many different story tellers. Just like the parlor game where someone whispers something in one ear, by the time it gets back to the author, it's changed somewhat. Of course, the idea was to recount the stories as accurately as possible. Given a few hundred or thousands of years, that accuracy may suffer a bit?

2,160 years was referred to as a great month by the Mayan. The age of Aquarius will last 2,160 years. 2,160 multiplied by 12 equals 25,920 years. That is what the Mayan called a great earth year. It takes the earth 25,920 years to complete one cycle of the wobble it takes with its axis. 216 doubled = 432. 432 multiplied by 60=25,920.

Did you know there are 432,000 seconds in 12 hours and 216,000 seconds in 6 hours? An ancient Indian time scale has 432,000 years in its cycle. 432,000 divided by 3 equals 144,000, which was the length of the Sumerian time scale. There are 144,000 chosen ones. There were 144,000 covering stones on the Great Pyramid. 144 is also the 12th iteration in the Fibonacci sequence.

In the Pythagorean secret theorem, the angles of the triangle are 36, 36 and 108. 108 doubled gives you 216. 36+36=72 It takes the earth 72 years to advance one degree of its 360-degree, 25,920-year wobble. 72 multiplied by 360= 25,920. There were 108 names for mother goddess in India. 72 doubled is 144.

Back in Pythagorean's day they took their secret theorems seriously. They murdered a man by drowning him for revealing the Pythagorean secret theorem. What made it so important? Did you know that the angles of the triangle in Pythagorean's theorem are the same as the dipole angles of a water molecule? All carbon-based life forms depend on water, or H_2O to exist.

If you take three of those triangles and fit them together you will get a five-pointed star, otherwise known as a pentagram. If you look at the center of that pentagram, it forms a pentagon. Kind of makes me wonder what the Mason's know?

Did you know, if you trace the visible pattern created by Venus, as seen from earth, it will create a pentagram, another sign post hint? Did you know that Mars orbit is equal to the radius of Saturn's orbit? Just a fun weird coincidental fact, or is it another sign post?

Why did the pentagram get associated with evil? Could it be because it was a very important piece of the cosmic puzzle and someone, or some being wanted their subjects not to look at it? Knowledge is power and that is why it is viewed as a threat to the power seekers. What easier way to keep your followers in line than to tell them a competing symbol is evil and they must obey the command to consider it evil. Those who don't must convert or be destroyed.

Of course, since it was labeled evil, people who do worship the dark side would adopt the pentagram as their symbol, enhancing the original instituted fears. The swastika was once a Buddhist symbol meaning "good fortune" and was seen as a symbol representing life and the sun. Then the symbol was adopted by the Nazis and perverted for their purposes.

A symbol's meaning can be altered slightly and used in drastically different ways than was originally conceived. The pentagram formed by configuring three Pythagorean triangles is just an expression of nature. It is only three water molecules configured together. You know, water, the giver of life.

A man named Carl Munck once had a dream he saw the construction of the Great Pyramid and received a message to "figure it out". They were quite persistent in sending him that message, even though he himself thought the task was above his abilities. He kept receiving the message "Do it!". He finally did it. I can absolutely relate to that.

What did Carl come up with? He discovered that there is a coded matrix connecting most of the major megalithic sites around the world.

This system utilizes the 12-inch foot and the 5,280-foot mile. It also utilizes the 360-degree circle with 60-minute degrees and 60 second increments, which is what modern navigation and cartography utilize.

In order for this matrix to be understood, Carl had to move the prime meridian from Greenwich England to the center of the Great Pyramid on the Giza plateau. The prime meridian is 0 degrees, 0 minutes, 0 seconds longitude. It is the starting point for computing any longitude on earth. Carl's moving of the prime meridian to the Giza Plateau resulted in the discovery of some amazing world-wide synchronicities. He found that the encoded matrix has a starting point in Bimini at the shark mound and goes from there across the globe. It is vast and a bit tedious, so I will only show you a few connections in this book.

He began his quest by studying Stonehenge and how it relates to the Great Pyramid. He first examined the site itself and found, for instance, that it had 30 upright stones and 30 crossing stones in a circle. 30+30=60 multiplied by 360=21,600. To Carl, the circle of stones represented a standard 360-degree circle. This same 360 degrees was encoded in every major megalithic site across the world.

The latitude of Stonehenge is 51 degrees, 10 minutes and 42.3529 seconds. Carl began to play with the numbers to see what he could come up with? Carl found that 21,600 divided by 51, divided by 10=423.5294118. Rounded off and changing the position of the decimal by one digit to the left will result in 42.3529. This shows that the latitude of Stonehenge is encoded. Since, 51 multiplied by 10 multiplied by 42.3529=21,600 rounded off. Carl referred to the sum of 21,600 as it's grid latitude. Stonehenge's longitude is 32 degrees 57 minutes 28.0173748 W. if it is calculated from the Giza prime meridian.

He went on finding ratios and connections to most of the megalithic sites across the world, while utilizing the Great Pyramid as the prime meridian. They seemed to be connected with very precise knowledge of the earth itself. In fact, we have only recently achieved the ability to be this precise with geographic measurements using modern technology. For instance, there is a site called the Octagon in Ohio that calculates a grid longitude of 216,000 utilizing Carl's method. There is no way humans could have had knowledge of the Earth's exact measurements when these sites were built? This was calculated utilizing the Great Pyramid as the prime meridian. So, how did this all get encoded across the earth? And when?

Carl Munck also investigated ancient numbers the Greeks called Gemetrian numbers. Back then numbers were considered more than numbers. They were viewed to have personalities, as if they were pseudo-living entities. Carl found that Romans and Mayans used the same numbers. Many of the numbers I have already mentioned are also gemetrian numbers. Gemetrian numbers add up to or multiply to 9 or are multiples of 9.

Carl found the Great Pyramid itself was encoded with gemetrian numbers that corelate with the speed of light. There are only two tangents for all gemetrian numbers if you ignore the – and + signs. A tangent is the ratio between the opposite side and adjacent side of a right-hand triangle.

The tangent of 72 is 3.077683537 and the tangent of 36 is 0.726542528. If you multiply those tangents, you get 2.236067977. Which is, coincidently, the square root of 5. The tangent of the square root of 5 equals 186,234.09485. That is the speed of light, in miles per second going through air as opposed to the speed of light through a vacuum which is slightly faster at 186,282.5894 miles per second.

I also want to mention the number 153. That number is encoded in the pyramid complex of Giza. 1+2+3+4+5+6+7+8+9+10+11+12+13+14+15+16+17=153.

There are 153 pyramids in total at the Giza complex that are without tombs. The entrance to the Great Pyramid is on the north side at the level of 153 courses. The length of the great gallery in the Great pyramid is 153 feet long. Let's try switching the three digits of 153 around and see what we find by doing some math? 153+513=666, 315+352=666, 135+531=666. Then of course, 6 multiplied by 6 multiplied by 6=216. 153 is one more link to the ubiquitous 216.

If you'd like to read a really good summation of Carl Munck's work I would suggest one done by Joseph E. Mason. Carl Munck also made videos that are posted on YouTube. https://youtu.be/oVejksVkqkk

If you are in a hurry my suggestion is to watch Carl Muncks first 40 minutes of the first video in the series and then skip to the last 30 minutes of his 3rd video on the matrix. All the other stuff is interesting for someone like me, but I know most might find the several hours of iteration boring.

In his book The Golden Vortex, Nick Nelson discusses an easy way to make a scale model of the Great pyramid. First draw a circle, then divide that circle into six equal sections. Connect the points where the lines from the sections meet the edge of the circle to each adjacent point, which then become triangles. Take out two triangles and the extra paper of the circle beyond the remaining four triangles. Then push the four remaining 60-degree equilateral triangles together. What will result is a scale model of the Great Pyramid with a slope of 51.43 degrees.

The thought occurred to me that a snow flake forms six points. If you connect the points then you form equilateral triangles radiating out from the center of a perfectly formed water crystal. By taking out two sections of that crystal and squeezing the remaining triangles together a perfect model of the Great Pyramid is formed. Perhaps another reference to water? Or the utilization of a universal geometric truth?

In the best-selling book, The Hidden Messages in Water, Masaru Emoto describes his experiments with water crystals. In one experiment he has participants project love or hate into a glass of water and then photographs the individual water crystals that are formed when that water is frozen. The crystals show that they morph into beautiful crystals when love is projected and are malformed when hate is projected into the water. Is H_2O a major key to all of this?

David Wilcock talks about history repeating itself every 2,160 years in his best-selling book, The Synchronicity Key. For instance, he compares Hannibal to Hitler in both character and appearance. I found his book a very good read, but I won't go into it because I will only include measurements of scale and time in this book. Nobody can argue with the fact that 6 multiplied by 6 multiplied by 6=216. People can disagree with the level of similarity of appearances and the repetition of similar historical events.

CHAPTER 10

Home Is Where The Heart Is

I HAVE BEEN in my house for over thirty-five years. I actually had two opportunities to buy it. Once, a realtor friend attempted to show it to me and I declined. Then, sometime later, a co-worker told me about a really good buy across the street from where he lives. It turned out to be the same house. I bought it in November of 1984, for the price of $26,500. It was a good buy. A two-bedroom house with an unfinished addition, that was built in 1955 and came with .7 acres. It sits on top of a knoll that drains on all sides, keeping it dry and resistant to rot.

Over the years I had it roofed once and then I bought the equipment and roofed it myself. I put a fifty-year roof on it, so it would outlive me. I've done numerous other things too. I'm not much for making it fancy. I'm a functional kind of guy. I just want it to be warm, dry and cozy, which it is.

It's located in a rural/suburb in the small town of Raymond, Washington. I live about four blocks from the edge of the woods and surrounding farmland. I have two lots, one of which is allowed to go pretty much wild. There are huge fir trees and some spruce and cedar I planted thirty years ago. I also have several other varieties of trees on my property.

In the summer the din of the birds can be deafening at times as several species collect in my trees. The six fir trees are the tallest in the neighborhood. The storms push them toward my house, but I don't care. I love my trees and I trust they will not smash me. They rode out the worst during the 2007 storm, which had winds of 120 miles an hour recorded less than five miles away.

As I write these words, I can look out the window and see the fir and spruce trees to the south. If I stand up and face east, I'm looking at the horizon where Orion can be seen on the winter solstice.

When I got back home from my trip to the Montana Vortex, I felt compelled to take out a map and begin to measure from the Montana vortex to my house. I had some old aviation sectionals left over from my flying days, but they were cumbersome and difficult to get accurate measurements. So, I went on Google Earth and used the ruler app on that site.

After trying a few things, I decided to measure a direct line from the Montana vortex to the vortex I was led to up in the Olympics. I noticed that line went 1.8 miles south of the Seattle vortex as charted by Nick Nelson. The center of the Seattle vortex is the center of Green Lake.

It measured 441 miles from the Montana vortex to what I now call the Olympic vortex. The Olympic vortex is 57 miles away from and 1.8 miles south of the center of the Seattle vortex. Then it measured 57 miles from the Olympic vortex to my home. After that, I checked the angle from the Seattle vortex to the Olympic vortex and down to my home. Checking the angle with a plotter on the screen of my computer, it appeared the angle was close enough to 114 degrees that is what I used. 57+57=114. Remember the number 327 I kept receiving? 441-327=114.

Much later, I decided to draw a line on a road map from my house to the Olympic vortex and then directly toward the Montana Vortex until it reached a canal that lies 1.8 miles directly south of the center of the Seattle Vortex field. Both lines are 57 miles long on the map. The center of the Seattle vortex is the center of Green Lake. I then drew a line back to my home from that point on the canal. It forms a triangle, of course. But, not just any triangle. The triangle that is formed appears to have the same angles as the triangle in Pythagorean's secret theorem, measuring 36, 36 and 108.

Eventually, I learned from watching Carl Munck that 57 is the radius of a 360-degree circle when 360 is used as the numerical number denoting its circumference. 360 divided by 2pi = 57 when rounded off.

It occurred to me that my house and the Seattle vortex lie on a 360-mile circle around the Olympic vortex with a 57-mile radius. I also noticed 327-216=111 and 432-327=105. 111 divided by 105= 1.057142875..... Notice there is a 57 and then it goes into the irrational number sequence usually only created by dividing 7 into numbers that aren't multiples of 7. There are so many strange links, it really struck me.

How did they set all of this up? It isn't always exact, but very close most of the time. When it isn't exact, the measurements usually end in an irrational number and need rounding off. Did they build the Olympic vortex before or after they guided me to my home? I believe the vortex fields were already in place long before they guided me to buy my house. It could have worked with another home nearby, but I don't think that was the plan? I was to have the perfect location with the kind of trees I love and a view of the east from my picture window. I am very lucky to have this wonderful, humble home and I thank them for it.

I'm not saying I was destined to be their pick for this particular assignment. Although, I wonder who else they would have picked? I do have some very unusual quirks in my personality they might have liked. I'm curious about the fundamentals of the universe, I'm a bit of a loner, though I have a thousand contacts with other humans, I'm a slow bloomer as far as emotional maturity goes, which contributed to me remaining single.

For me, it seems as though the metaphysical experiences put me on the path to complete my emotional maturity. I realized that death is an illusion and we are all connected and therefore compassion and love are the most important thing we can express. I began to own up to my own faults more. Believe me, I'm not perfect, who is?

This is what I mean when I say, I owe them. They have shown me the error of an overabundance of self-absorption, or the need to boost one's ego. It makes life so much easier when I don't want anything, except that moment in front of me. The ego is heavy baggage for people to lug around. Trying to feed it is a burden. It's funny saying that, because a strong ego is manifested on stage. A good actor or musician has confidence and wants to feed their ego. But on stage is one thing and normal, everyday life is another.

I appreciate the gift of a summer breeze and the bloom of a flower more than ever before. I have come to love my humble home and my humble life. I'm perfectly happy watching a bumble bee bounce from bloom to bloom.

Quite often I spend time on my back deck at night. I have a lounge chair, a cushy cushion and a sleeping bag that is good down to zero degrees. If it is clear and warmer than 20 degrees above zero, more than not, you can find me on my back deck at night. In fact, as I write this, I have been on my back deck for the last five nights in a row.

It is very pleasant on my back-deck gazing at the stars. It's a great way of topping off the day. I have an app on my phone that shows me the names of the stars, planets and constellations. Often, I fall asleep for a little while. I see the constellations, planets, commercial aircraft, meteors, aurora borealis, satellites, UFO's and UAP's. Wait, what!? UFO's and UAP's?

UFO stands for unidentified flying object and UAP stands for unidentified air phenomena. UAP is now the official term utilized by our government. The terms are interchangeable for us civilians.

I began to see UFO's around my house early in the year 2019. I heard, through the grapevine, that others in my neighborhood were seeing them too, including my next-door neighbor. We often exchange notes on what we've seen.

What have I seen? Various things that I would label UFO's or UAP's. A lot of time they just look like a bright satellite, except they will maneuver and not adhere to an orbital trajectory. Sometimes they flash and move around. They often disappear then reappear in another part of the sky. They also change color on occasion. I've seen orange, red, green, blue, yellow and usually white.

A few times I've seen what I would describe as white balls of fire that appear and disappear. They come in threes and fly in formation or at least in close proximity to each other. One time three white lights came in a formation which reminded me of the Pythagorean triangle. In fact, that was the night after I studied the secret theorem. Were they illustrating it for me?

I've learned to distinguish between commercial aircraft, meteors, satellites and other mundane human stuff and other not so mundane stuff. For instance, a satellite can be spinning and changing its brightness, appearing like flashes in the sky as a reflective panel presents itself to the sun. The International Space Station is very bright and so on... Conventional aircraft are easy to spot by their navigation lights.

Although I no longer pilot aircraft, I do still possess a pilot's license, because they never expire. I'm just not current, as they refer to it and therefore it would be illegal for me to pilot an aircraft without an instructor with me. I have logged over eleven hundred hours in the left seat of various aircraft. That gives me an advantage over most, when it comes to determining what conventional navigation lights are and what aren't. However, one morning while rinsing out my coffee cup I saw what at first appeared to be a conventional aircraft, except it was suspiciously too low and appeared to be hovering. So, I grabbed my binoculars and had a look. It turned out that the lights were near the middle of the aircraft and it was disk shaped. I could see its silhouette just above the early morning eastern horizon. The lights were near the middle and its structure, which spread out in both directions' way beyond those lights. It was gigantic! I ran to get my phone and rushed out to my front lawn to record it. By the time I got out there, it was gone. I figure it took me less than ten seconds to get out there with my phone. It disappeared quickly, as if it knew my plan?

About ten minutes after I saw the mother ship, I went on line and ordered a somewhat fancy Cannon XA 11 with HD quality and infra-red capability. Infra-red picks up the heat signature of an object. Soon after it arrived, I was outdoors next to my house, attempting to record some UFO activity when I heard someone walk up on my right side, only about ten feet away. I turned to look, but saw nothing because it was too dark? Then I realized I had a camera with infra-red capability in my hands, so I swung it around to see what I could see? I saw nothing. I'm sure there was someone there, but I couldn't see him.

I do have some anomalies recorded that were moving around one night. In fact, I went out to record a lightning storm I could see to the east soon after I received my camera via mail. I inadvertently recorded some strange, fast moving and colorful lights in the valley. I didn't notice them until I reviewed my recording. So far, I haven't had much luck at recording the really good ones. Usually, when I see something spectacular, it is fleeting and only appears for a few seconds.

Recently, I saw a single bright flash that was yellow with red in the middle. I often see flashes that appear to be saying "hello" to me. I've also seen green ones. Why would I think they are saying hello? A few months ago, I saw what looked like balls of flame that would appear and then flame out. It occurred three times in quick succession, each appearing parallel to the one before. They were right above me. I thanked them for the show and got a flash straight above, as if they were saying, "You're welcome." That has happened a few times.

Inside the house I hear movement, quite often. I also have seen shadows and lights. My neighbor even hears something in his house once in a while. He tells me he will wake up and hear footsteps and then his door will close. He'll get up and look outside and nothing is there? His house was built in the thirties and I'm wondering if it has its own hauntings, or if my house has some influence?

I experience these weird events so often that I've become somewhat immune to them. One night I woke up while I had my leg out from under the covers. I then felt a push on my big toe. I thought it was my cat, before realizing my cat was sucked up against my back. I was too tired and not in the mood, so without opening my eyes, I pulled my foot back under the covers and went back to sleep, without even looking.

Around this time, I was in my bathroom one morning and noticed an odd print on the bathmat that was very small. It looked like it was wearing a sock and its longest toe was in the middle.

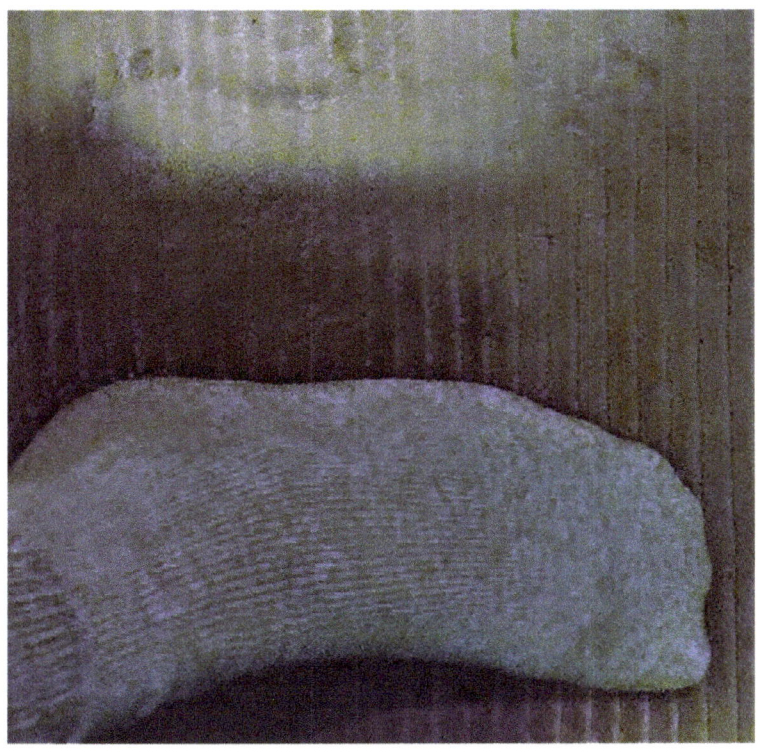

Another night I was watching a baseball game and received, what gave me the impression. of a down load into my brain. It went on for several minutes. Soon after I went to a UFO summit in Ocean Shores, Washington and talked to Darrel Simms, The UFO Hunter, about it. He told me that is a common experience among abductees. Yikes!

One evening it was too warm in the house, so I opened the sliding glass door in my bedroom about six inches to cool it off before bedtime. Then I went back into the living room and watched tv for a bit. After about a half hour I crawled into bed and began meditating with all of the several gifts of crystal and agate I've received. I was lying on my back and had been meditating for about ten minutes when my cat jumped up on my bed. Immediately, I felt what I would describe as a tiny elbow against the heel of my foot. I instinctively pulled my foot back from the pressure. Whatever it was took off and exited the bottom of the bed. I opened my eyes and saw my cat lunge for it, as if she didn't really want to catch it. I sat up quickly to see what it was, but missed it? It had already slipped out of the sliding glass door and down the steps of my back deck. All I thought I saw, for an instant, was a transparent, eight to twelve-inch-tall brown something? Mind you I did not have me glasses on. That was very weird. I had something with me, in my bed, below my feet, for several minutes without knowing it.

One morning I woke up before dawn to what appeared to be a portal? It was in the northwest corner of my bedroom. It was a quarter of a circle and I assume the other three quarters were outside the bedroom. I estimate it extended one cubit (25 inches) from the corner of my room. It had a black boarder that was approximately $1/6^{th}$ the diameter of that circle, if indeed it was a circle. A vortex has a corona $1/6^{th}$ the diameter of its circumference.

I got up and took a close look. I really was at a loss as to what it was or why it was there? I then turned on the lights and it faded. I turned the lights back off and it appeared as before. It had its own luminescence and glowed with an enigmatic, dark and beautiful radiant blue. I wasn't at all afraid of it. I knew it came in peace and with love. This, I instinctively understood. Then again, I wasn't about to stick my hand in it, either. I finally gave up on it and went in and started the coffee. When I returned, it was gone.

That incident reminded me of one I had years before in another house I was renting. I just happened to be living at the bottom of the hill where I had my first recognizable sasquatch encounter, with strong odor and knocks in 2011. This incident took place in the early 1980's. I had woke up early in the morning to an orange orb hovering above me. I first thought it might be a light from my clock radio, but that wasn't the case. Then I noticed that it was in the shadow made by the window in the morning light and therefore the origin was not from outdoors. As soon as I came to the conclusion that it was a light in and of itself, it faded away and disappeared. I got the impression that it was objectively observing me, with no nefarious agenda. Knowing what I know now, I believe it was probably my sasquatch teacher. Recently I found an interpretation of an orange orb, according to what I could find it means teacher.

I finally purchased an EMF (Electromagnetic frequency meter) that is supposed to detect spirits. If I turn it on in my house it will, sooner or later, light up like a Christmas tree on almost any given day. Home sweet home. I actually don't mind all of the attention and company. It is both comforting and fun, even to the extent of being comedic at times.

Sometime in the early 2000's, I had Russell and his ex, house sit for me. He told me a jar flew off of the drainboard, flew across the kitchen and hit the stove, twice. I kind of think they didn't like his ex? When he told me that story, I was still a skeptic and didn't believe him. I assumed there must be some kind of "rational" explanation for it. Wow, have I changed my tune.

One night I was meditating and sending my hello's and love down through the ground and out to all of nature. I'm always thankful for my wonderful life and nature. Something followed my message back home. At first, I heard something under my bed and thought it must be my cat. My cat had never played under the bed before. I could hear it scratching and then the noise got very frantic and too intense to be my cat. At this time, I was lying on my right side with my left knee bent and lifted.

I decided I needed to reach for the flashlight I always keep on the night stand and shine a light on whatever it was? Just as I had that thought, it came up through the bed, lifted the mattress and my leg, flipping me onto my back. As soon as I was flipped onto my back and staring at the blank ceiling, I knew it was over. The whole thing took place in less than thirty seconds and didn't even raise my heart beat. Something about that entity seems familiar to me now. Could it have been the one that jumped out of the shaman stone or crystal heart?

Whatever it was had followed my message back to my house and had come up through the floor, only to get temporarily stuck under my bed. The mattress is on a plywood board. So somehow, it came through the plywood and lifted the mattress? I'm also thinking that the plywood board might have surprised and temporarily confused my visitor?

I have projected myself down and out to nature during meditation since, but have had no such re-occurrence. It could have been what some call an elemental? Who knows? It also could have been a demonstration showing that they do listen and hear me when I send them a message while meditating.

One of the things you attempt to do when interacting with any of this is stay calm. In fact, many paranormal investigators will say that an evil entity will feed on fear. It could be that your electromagnetic energy is ramped up when you are fearful. It appears that electromagnetic energy is what spirits feed on to manifest.

Am I afraid? I believe I might be in some danger? Not from my teacher, or any entities he is associated with. There are those entities that aren't so nice lurking about our planet. I've decided not to be afraid of the unknown. I trust my teacher and all of this has come from him and his connections to other beings from other worlds and or realms. They have shown me nothing less than total love and devotion. In fact, at times I'm overwhelmed at how much effort they have put into guiding me along the way. Besides, if you can get past the fear all the wonders of the universe open up to you. Also, I believe I'm being watched over very carefully, twenty-four hours a day. That does make me wonder what they are protecting me from?

I know a man who has been attacked twice by unseen entities. He said sasquatch showed up and protected him both times. He is sure he would be dead now, if they hadn't come to his rescue.

Why did they want to kill him? Steve Bachman built a Tesla coil and he utilized it at an active portal to give it strength to facilitate a mass migration. Orbs came pouring through the portal from a dying planet. The orbs were sasquatch. He said over twenty thousand came through and are now on our planet. Does that explain why there's been a dramatic uptick in sasquatch sightings?

Obviously, there are entities that didn't appreciate him helping so many of their enemy come through. Who Might that be? I'm not going to point a finger, because I really am not sure who they are? I just know they are.

It wasn't that long ago, I thought the claim that they brought so many through a portal, questionable? I did go to the big reveal where Dr. Mathew Johnson talked about what they had done and found a lot of it somewhat plausible, but I wasn't convinced. When I talked to Steve Bachmann one on one, I believed him. Knowing what I know now, it seems very plausible. He helped sasquatch and now they are committed to make sure he does not suffer because of it. That really is the way they are. They are dedicated friends.

I've had my forest buddies up in the Olympics chase off intruders at least twice, that I know of? The first time I was in my tent, up around

Lake Wynootchee, when I heard what sounded like coyote around the perimeter whining as if they wanted something? They were very persistent and I thought it might be me they wanted and it made me uneasy. Before long I heard Jacque and the gang arrive and the coyote were silenced and gone, instantly.

That time was on me, because I had bought a huge sandwich which I couldn't finish. I had placed it on top of a stump and forgot about it. I'm sure the coyote could smell it, but were reluctant to go get it, because they didn't want to come down off the ridge and get that close to my camp.

One day I lost my keys in a swim hole at the eye of the Olympic vortex. I spent all afternoon looking for them. The water was crystal clear, but filled with softball sized rocks. The keys had slipped in between those rocks and I couldn't find them. I grabbed a big limb and spent all afternoon moving the large rocks around, but that only stirred up sediment and made it impossible to find my keys. The Subaru was locked, because I had been doing some exploring.

Fortunately, I had already set up the hammock with my sleeping bag in it. After spending several hours attempting to find my keys I was glad I had a place to sleep. While lying there in my hammock, awaiting the sand man to come, I heard a cougar scream from just a few yards away. I wasn't nervous at all. I could tell the cougar was being chased off and that was why it screamed. So, I rolled over on my side and went to sleep without a care in the world. I knew the next day would be a long one, but I didn't worry about it. After all, what would worrying about it at that point in time do for me? The mosquitoes were a little annoying, because I had no access to my deet insect repellent, but other than that it was a very pleasant evening and I enjoyed it.

I've put out an overnight recorder at this location before and picked up a rustle and exhale from one of my friends. I have also had them there when I played my guitar. They really do watch over me out there, probably more than I know?

The next day I got up just as it was getting light out. I went down to the river and took several large drinks of water and headed out. I had to wear my wet water moccasins for the hike out and it wasn't long before I was stuffing leaves into my footwear to try and cushion my feet and stop the bleeding. Fortunately, two fisherman/bear hunters, originally from Montana, picked me up and took me thirteen miles out of their way to a junction where I could hitch a ride. I had my fold up backpacking camp chair and I was wearing a yellow striped beach shirt with green swimsuit, sunglasses and no form of ID. What a picture I must have made while I worked my way 87 road miles back to my home, via Aberdeen.

My neighbor saw me get dropped off and came over to find out what had happened? I told him and he went and got his keys and drove me all the way back up there to get my Subaru. I managed to get back home with my rig just as it was getting dark. Nice neighbor!

I wonder now if that was a lesson? Did they cause that to happen? I was in the water up to my knees with my keys in my pocket and knew I had to be careful. A huge deer fly came and began to hassle me and without thinking I jumped into the deep part of the swim hole to escape that little demon. That is when the keys found their way out of my pocket. Did they somehow direct that fly? I had been getting more and more cynical towards human beings. Perhaps that was a way to get me to lighten up a little? I have slowly come to realize that they can manipulate a wide diversity of outcomes and people.

On my journey back home, I was helped by people from the left, right and middle of the political spectrum as well as various races and ethnic groups. All were so kind and generous to give me rides and a little money even, since I didn't have any to buy a bottle of water. That true adventure and journey renewed my faith in humanity. There was one man, with his family in the car with him, that gave me an unkind gesture while I was hitchhiking. Other than that, I made out quite well. It took me three hitched rides and two buses to get back home.

I feel a great devotion to the project, whatever it is? I believe it has something to do with a reveal to humanity and/or knowledge of portals and how they get around from one planet to the next? I've attempted to be a good student and work hard toward the culmination and completion of my part in the mission.

In 2019 I had mastered down all of my songs from the musical I wrote onto a CD, in order to license them with CD Baby. I had put the master CD into a small CD player to check out the songs and make sure everything was copasetic. When it got to one song the volume went way up. I wondered how I could have made such a mistake and played the whole CD again? This time everything seemed fine. After listening to it for three times without incident, I came to the conclusion that they were messing with the electronics as a joke. I was very tired from all the work I had put in that day. I really wasn't in the mood and sent them that message. I told them to let up please and that I would probably laugh at their joke later, but not that day.

Early in 2020 I was meditating and suddenly it came to me that they were attempting to bring my attention to that particular song. It was out of sequence. I didn't understand that at the time and now my CD has one song that is out of order with the sequence of songs in the play. It's really not that big of a deal, but I do wish they were in perfect order. That incident informed me how closely they watch me. Many people would be creeped out by that, not me.

I've come to believe that none of us are ever alone. There are entities of various types right here, right now that I can't see. They are around you right now, as well. They usually lurk in dimensions that are currently beyond our comprehension and detection. Think in terms of a television set. There are 2D images of people on the tv that we can see, but they can't see us. We are in a 3D world and there are those who can see us, but we can't see them. At least, most of us can't see them.

Our vision is limited to one octave of the electromagnetic spectrum. I now believe that sensitives who can see ghosts might have a larger spectrum of vision on the high side of the visual spectrum? Below the visual spectrum you have infra-red and above it shifts blue within the electromagnetic spectrum. I also know that we all suffer from subjective filters that our brains utilize to form our perceptions. If something does not jive with our belief system then it is not seen, or accepted.

When Columbus first arrived in the western hemisphere in the year 1492, most of the natives couldn't see the ships. Only the shaman could see them and had to convince the others that they were indeed there and real. Our brain has a huge capacity for cognitive dissonance that most of us aren't even aware of.

Our brains categorize familiar things we see in order to help us recognize what we are seeing. When we see a house, for instance, our brain checks for familiar components of what we are viewing. It's called principal component analysis.

Plato described humans utilizing only two characteristics. According to Plato we are bipedal, with no feathers. Hopefully, most of us utilize more components for recognizing humans? The brain scrolls down for recognizable components and then decides what the eye is seeing. This function is going on in different parts of the brain. In the case of the natives not seeing Columbus upon his arrival their brains had trouble trying to compute what they were seeing, because the components of the sailing ships were unfamiliar. The shaman could see them, because a shaman is open and used to novel encounters with spirits and various phenomena.

One night after a dress rehearsal I was sitting quietly on my couch with my cat on my lap, thinking about how well the rehearsal went. There was only one LED light coming from my space heater. I saw a shadow walk the length of my living room right in front of me. I'm thinking that was a sasquatch, but I really am not sure? It did make me smile to myself. If I'd had any lights on, other than that single LED light, I would not have seen that shadow. So, how often does that occur?

I was hiking one day up near where I experienced the Mandela effect. It was a beautiful, crisp, winter day with sun and absolutely calm winds. I suddenly felt a warm whirlwind come up right around me. I could smell very fragrant flowers, even though there were none around at that time of the year. I then felt something penetrate the left side of my head. I knew it was my teacher, but I did not know what he had injected into my brain?

Apparently, the job wasn't done yet, because later that evening I felt the same penetration while sitting on the couch with my cat curled up on my lap. My cat's head snapped up and swiveled around to look at me with eyes as big as saucers, as if to ask "What was that!?" I gave her a pet and told her it was alright and she went back into her dream state. I still have no idea what that was about?

My cat is the canary in the cave. One day she was sitting on my lap and we both heard what sounded like a squeak toy coming from the corner of my living room. That corner is where some of my guitar cases lean against the wall creating a cubby hole underneath that she likes to go into sometimes.

Little Grr, as I call her, jumped off of my lap and went over to where the sound emanated from. She couldn't see or find anything and looked back at me for instruction or direction or explanation? I shrugged my shoulders and told her, "Who knows? I have no idea what that was little Grrr?". Quite often she will react to something I can't even detect. So, when her attention is aroused, I try and pay attention.

My friend Jill Smith bought a private campsite north of Elma, Washington early in 2019. When Jill first looked at the property, she saw a female and male sasquatch walk through, only about thirty feet away. They did no look at her. She knew it was a message telling her to buy that property. She told me when she saw them "I knew the property was meant for me." I felt compelled to visit as soon as possible.

My first trip was a community camp out with a few other friends of Jill's that are involved with the sasquatch phenomena. There was a couple by the names of Keith and Dawn already there when I showed up. They are very nice and I hope to see them again sometime. While they were there I decided to go meditate and pray with my shoulders pressed between two old cedar trees. When I returned the few yards back to where we were sitting, Dawn told me that there must be a ley line that cuts through those cedar trees. She said she could see powerful waves of energy radiating from my body in a rush as I stood there.

Then Dawn took me and showed me where the line is. She took me to one tree and put her hand on it. Then he told me to do the same. I could feel the power coursing through my hand. I took my hand off of the tree and the power went away, then I placed my hand back on the tree and could feel it again. I was surprised, amazed and happy that I could feel it too. That tree and the one next to it bears scars from a lightning strike. Is lightning drawn to a ley line?

The bushmen of the Kalahari Desert in Africa can see ley lines. When my friend Adam Davies, the famous cryptozoologist, was hanging out with them he asked how they could find the villages, because the land is so lacking in landmarks? They told him they build their villages on ley lines and then they just follow the ley lines to the various villages. They were surprised to learn that he could not see them.

I believe this is an ability that we have lost or forgotten about? It has been tamped down with modernity. Ley lines are no longer something most our brains recognize. No need to see or follow a ley line when you have a well-defined interstate highway system. Recently, I detected a ley line or demarcation line as I was hiking. Perhaps I'm becoming more sensitive to magnetic anomalies? It felt heavy for about two steps as I crossed the line. It was only then that I realized I was one road over and just a few hundred yards from where I experienced the Mandela effect lesson. Since that first detection, I've crossed that line several times without being able to feel it again?

Later, I discussed woo with another camp goer who showed up at the campsite on that same trip. I mentioned how UFOs were linked with sasquatch. He said that isn't true. I said, "Well, you might not believe it's true, but it is a fact." Not much after that, he was the first to see a UFO that night. I must admit some real satisfaction in that. Did they show up to support my assertion? I would not doubt it. Sasquatch came later as it began to get dark and we heard them and could see eye shine.

What we saw that night were orbs that floated above the horizon to the south. They hung around for several minutes, if not hours. They were a little brighter than stars and acted like balloons that rose and fell and moved right and left a few degrees.

One lady was beside herself and feeling a lot of fear over the UFO's. She didn't seem to be bothered by sasquatch? I tried to calm her fears by telling her, "This is the universe as it is. We've all been sheltered from this truth our whole lives. There is nothing to fear." I don't think my words helped much as she continued to shake like a leaf. She was ready for sasquatch, but this was something unexpected and new to deal with.

I can relate to her reluctance. I remember thinking when the UFOs showed up that they might be related to the sasquatch phenomena and I wasn't very excited about ETs entering the mix. I remember sending out the message, "Okay, I'm only going to deal with the sasquatch, NO ETs!" My position has softened considerably since.

I also spent solo time there and heard sasquatch every night. During the day I would hike around looking for any kind of sign. I did find this very interesting teepee, pictured below. These kinds of structures are very rare in this part of the continent. They are common in other parts. There do seem to be cultural differences from location to location. It could also be a conscious decision about what they want to convey to the local human population?

I took my friend Russell Wilson there and we saw more UFO's and heard sasquatch. For the most part the UFOs we saw seemed to hang above that ley line most of the time. They were multi colored and streaky. As it was getting dark that night, I saw a rainbow pattern for a moment just a few feet away from me. Then as we sat, late at night, we both saw a double band grey wave come over our heads. I have not spent a night there yet when something hasn't happened.

One-night Jill took a picture of a UFO directly above the campsite that had a ring of lights.

Jill Smith shot this through a canopy of trees above the campsite. The lights are clearly visible.

After getting home I felt compelled to open up Google earth and check the distance from my house to the campsite. Her property is exactly 36 miles from my home, as the crow flies.

Shortly before I left to go to the campsite for the first time, I had been reviewing how electrons have to travel 720-degrees to complete one 360 degree round trip as they travel the figure eight mobius route. My thought was that I had traveled to her campsite and that was 360 degrees and a visit to the other side. Then I returned to my home completing the 720-degree full cycle. I now consider myself a human electron. According to Ken Wheeler an electron is merely a magnetic field and not a particle. So, I guess I'm really a reciprocating magnetic hyperbola.

Jill Smith has been allowed to take pictures of sasquatch. She has several, but par the course, most are blurry. Zoomed in, this one from 2015 is one of her best. It was not taken at her private campsite.

One eye, the brow line, cheek line, conical head and nostrils all can be seen. Jill believes it's a she?

I do believe they might be more willing to show themselves to a woman. Jill sees them much more often than I. Almost every time I've seen them, it seems to be very well orchestrated and very brief. Other than eye shine at Jill's campsite, I haven't seen one for three years now. I'm not worried about it. I'm sure I haven't seen my last sasquatch. In fact, I might have seen one a few months ago. I was hiking and heard a knock. I then saw a black something, that was very fast, streak across a spur road. The road had tall sword ferns growing on it, so it obscured that jet-black animal. There are only two black animals to choose from, other than a sasaquatch? One is a bear and the other is a skunk. The bear would be recognizable as a small cub and where was the sow? Also, I think it was too fast to be a skunk.

Yes, these photos are what many call blobsquatches. But we are only going to get what they gift us. All of the blurry pictures might be due to their vibrational abilities? I have seen crystal clear photos of them, but that is so rare.

Can you see the face? It appears to me that the face changes positions slightly in this series of photos.

Let me remind you again to pay very little attention to the zeroes with all of this. Zeroes don't seem to count when it comes to sacred math. 36+36=72. 72 degrees being very important number in Pythagorean's secret theorem. Let it be noted that the earth's axis advances one degree every 72 years on its journey to wobble 360 degrees. Also, if you take the diameter of the sun at 864,000 miles and the diameter of the earth at 7,920 miles, then remove the zeroes. 864-792=72

It amazes me how many of these strange synchronistic correlations exist. Some of these things I've found just through persistence. I'm also guided to information that they then confirm through demonstration, or a well-placed piece of evidence. I'm continually impressed by how clever the unfolding is and how timely. It's as if I've been placed in a slow-moving epic movie, unfolding over the years. I'm not unhappy about it. I always look forward to the next scene. "All the world is a stage and all men and women are players" after all. That being a quote I actually had the pleasure of uttering on stage once during an amateur production of, As You Like It. Another great quote of Shakespeare's "There are stranger things in heaven and on earth than are dreamt of in your philosophies."

CHAPTER 11

Nicola Tesla

"The day science begins to study non-physical phenomena; it will make more progress in one decade than in all the previous centuries of its existence."
Nikola Tesla

IN EARLY 2019, I was watching a program on Nicola Tesla. In one scene they showed the hallway door to what for decades was his apartment. Much to my surprise I found his apartment number was identical to the number I was given, 327. He actually resided in apartment 3327, but I don't count the first number because it designates the story his former apartment is on. In other words, he lived on the third floor, apartment 327.

The next morning, I went to the playhouse for a board meeting. I decided to meet in the big dressing room and found a piece of paper to write a message to alert the attendees. When I picked up the piece of paper, I noticed something was written on the back of it. I turned it over and there was one word, "Tesla". What are the odds, right?

I actually know who wrote that word. One young man in a play I was directing is fascinated by the Tesla vehicle and drew the logo on that paper with the name. None the less, I picked it up off the lobby desk and recognized it was being utilized to convey another message.

At this point I'd experienced their signals enough times that I immediately accepted the idea that they wanted me to study Tesla. Especially since I knew that Nicola Tesla was interested in all things magnetic and electric. I also knew that he had some metaphysical experiences over the span of his life.

I bought a couple of books, one on his inventions and patents and the other was his biography. Then I went on line to see what I could find about this mysterious and fascinating genius.

Nikola Tesla (1856-1943) was really the man responsible for our ubiquitous, worldwide use of alternating electric current. In fact, he essentially invented our modern world when he invented the alternating current induction motor. He also invented the famous Tesla coil which is utilized in radio transmission.

He was a brilliant man who held the patent on 112 inventions in the U. S. alone. All together he held 196 patents in 26 different countries. Most of his patents could have made him a lot of money, except he was preoccupied with his work. So, administratively and motivationally he was an inept capitalist. His true motivation was to help mankind, a virtuous and somewhat rare motive this day and age.

Tesla was also known to be somewhat eccentric. For instance, he would always walk around the apartment building he lived in three times before entering.

Tesla believed his most important discovery by far was his discovery of alternating magnetic fields. He felt that all his other inventions of gadgets and motors will be superseded, but the significance of his discovery of rotating magnetic fields would live on forever. He knew that he would be recognized more for his work in the future than by his contemporaries, because his discoveries were cutting edge. That future is here.

In case you haven't noticed, Nicola Tesla has been receiving more attention recently than in the last few decades. People are beginning to recognize and study his genius. I recently saw estimates of the highest I.Q.s of historical figures throughout recorded history. Tesla made that short list with an estimated I.Q between 180 and 220.

While online, looking for anything about Tesla, I came across Theoria Apophasis, A.K.A. Ken Wheeler. He is a big fan of Tesla's and rejects particle physics as Tesla did. Ken claims to have come up with the unifying theory while studying Pythagorean's secret theorem. I began to study ken's videos on magnetism and eventually watched him explain his unifying theory. It took more than one watch of his videos before I got it. When I did, I felt an instant surge of joy in knowing something that so few understand. I can only imagine how charged up Ken was when he first realized his discovery? For me it was a struggle and then it clicked instantaneously, like an explosion. I knew, objectively, that he was correct in his assertions. What I am now asserting is that Ken Wheeler is the first human to discover the unifying theory.

In one of Ken's videos, he discusses a friend of his who patented one of Tesla's ideas for wireless high-power voltage transmission. Ken explained how it worked and I found it rather interesting. It requires the receiving station to be in line of site with the transmitter or relay station. Sort of like widely spread telephone poles, except without the wires. The electricity moves from one pole to the next via something called scaler waves. The way laser beams focus is similar to the way scaler waves would move from pole to pole. They move in a direct line and stay confined to a beam.

Right after learning about this new patent, I went to the playhouse to help ready for a showing of my musical, Haunted Hannan Playhouse. Often, I get a little over exuberant when I learn a new thing and I began to tell three people in the lobby about it. While I was talking about it Linda plugged in the coffee maker and Liz, who was halfway across the lobby, began to complain of a very sharp pain in her foot. I looked at the coffee maker and then checked out where Liz was standing and then I looked back at the coffee maker. I realized that Liz was in direct view of the coffee maker. Liz saw the way I was examining her position, relative to the coffee maker and got the hint and told Linda to unplug the coffee maker. Linda unplugged the coffee maker and Liz' foot stopped hurting. Then Linda plugged it back in and Liz' foot began to sting again, so Linda unplugged it and threw the coffee maker away. I tried to explain to Linda that "they" were demonstrating what I had just learned, but she didn't want to hear it.

The next day at the playhouse Linda told us she had figured out what had happened the day before. I asked for details and she said she had figured out that we had hoaxed her. The other two ladies that were there the night before for that demonstration, informed her it wasn't a hoax. The look on Linda's face was priceless. She had come face to face with metaphysics and it was shaking her denial system to the core. Obviously, she had given it considerable thought overnight.

A few months later Linda would see 25 UFOs diverge above our town in a star pattern. She said her whole paradigm is shifting. Sometimes, that is what it takes.

The other thing I found interesting about Ken Wheeler was the fact that he'd seen UFOs more than once. When I learned that, I had the thought that he might be another "chosen" human being?

Ken teaches that every, so called sub-atomic particle, except for protons, are magnetic fields and not particles. According to Ken Wheeler everything in the universe is made up of different forms of magnetism. Therefore, the formula for the unifying theory, $1/phi$ cubed, is simple and universal. It describes the structure of every magnetic field in the universe.

Ken wheeler is an interesting fellow. He is a professional photographer and posts reviews on various camera models. He is also a translator of ancient languages, with an acute interest in and knowledge of metaphysics.

Ken owns the patent on over two hundred of his original ideas. I know hardly anything about his patents? I do know he has over two hundred patents more than I've got. He's not a fan of Einstein and calls him an idiot. Now before you get all bent out of shape, consider how Tesla essentially said the same thing about Einstein only in more colorful terms. Ken is ready to point out that Tesla invented our modern world and Einstein invented nothing. Tesla referred to Einstein's math as "magnificent mathematical garb which fascinates, dazzles and makes people blind to the underlying errors." Einstein, along with many others, got caught up in the particle wave that hit physics. Ken calls it the "Cult of bumping particles."

Tesla vehemently disagreed with Einstein's notion that space could bend and therefore cause gravity. Tesla said it is impossible to bend space, because it has no attributes. Ken Wheeler says to think of space as you would a shadow, which is merely an absence of light and has no attributes of its own. Also, Tesla knew the medium we call ether was a real thing that particle physicists were and still are ignoring. Tesla said "There is no energy in the environment other than that received from the environment." I believe he was referencing the ether.

In the eighteenth century, John Dalton came up with the idea that everything, even on its tiniest scale is a particle. Eventually that theory led to particle physics. The math of particle and quantum physics is super complicated, unwieldly and leaves a lot of questions left to be answered. Ken Wheeler believes it is a cultish type of science that is perpetuated through the cultish devotion of its followers. The structure of that cult is so ingrained and institutionalized in our academia it has become near impossible to dislodge. It turns out that even scientists can be very subjective and like Schrödinger's cat, stuck in a box.

Even before I found Ken, I was wondering about the discovery of the so-called god particle, otherwise known as the Higgs Boson? How could a particle impart mass on an object? Wouldn't it need some kind of field to do that? According to Ken the answer, found through platonic logic, is yes and that is the magnetic field.

What is the nature of the tiny packet of light known as the photon in particle physics? A photon, according to quantum physics, is supposedly a duality, meaning it is both a particle and a wave at the same time. Really? It is an explanation that works for their complicated calculations and experiments, or maybe it doesn't? To me it's sort of like attempting to toast ice.

Actually, light crosses the universe as a wave. Waves need some kind of medium to move through. If you try and create a wave with your hand in a bathtub it will only work if there is a medium in it, in other words, water. So, what is the universal medium? There has to be one because a wave is not a particle. It is a perturbation of a medium, otherwise known as the ether.

It goes by different names: Ether, zero-point field, inertial field, counter space and so on…. As Shakespeare once said, "A rose by any other name would smell as sweet." Call it what you will, it is the same thing.

The universe is full of waves Criss crossing our universe. If all the light of all the stars are Criss crossing the universe as particles or "dualities", then why don't we see the light as it travels through space?

Light from the brightest star in the universe only shows itself when it hits something, such as the back of a human eyeball. If you turn around and face the opposite way from a super nova explosion you will not see the light going past you, fading into the distance. You will only see blackness until you turn and face the light.

If photons are particles, or "dualities", then why can't you catch and collect them in some way? You can't fill an empty container by opening the lid and letting the light shine in because photons aren't particles, nor are they dualities. Quantum photons don't exist. There are only light waves traveling in a universal ocean, or bathtub of ether.

The human eye can only see about one octave of the full spectrum of wavelengths. Anything outside that spectrum we can't see. The ether is not a wave and is undetectable by any eye or instrument. We can only detect those waves that traverse the ether when they bump up against something and not the ether itself. Because a wave needs some kind of medium to travel through, it only makes sense that the ether does exists and permeates everything. It is, in a sense, the invisible, undetectable water in our cosmic tub. Empty space is not empty.

In the spring of 2019, I was hiking about ten miles from my house. I spied an ex, I thought it beautiful and took a picture. I was hiking up in this area again, because I was sure they were responsible for a structure I had found up there a few weeks before. A few minutes later, while hiking, I felt something big come from my left side. The first instant of detection I thought it was an elk. I had experienced elk and deer jumping out right in front of me before. It angled from my left rear to my front right side of my body at a 45-degree path and it was very close and fast. I could feel its mass change the air pressure on my face as it ran by, but I saw nothing!? Then I heard a crack in the woods ahead and to the right.

He was right there, yet I couldn't see him? This was obviously another lesson from my teacher. A lesson in cloaking. I stood there for about a minute waiting for a further sound or movement. None came, so I continued on my hike.

Visible light occupies one octave in the same section of frequencies as electromagnetism. In fact, interesting enough, the ratio of electromagnetic spectrum to visible light is equal to phi or 1.618.

Sasquatch: Shaman of the Woods

I've heard people talk about how sasquatch raises the level of his or her frequency when they disappear. The higher the frequency the greater the power. The sasquatch was glowing brightly inside the Montana House of Mystery in the recording and Joe wasn't when he entered, just a few minutes later. I believe the sasquatch was glowing because he was emitting light at a higher, more powerful frequency.

Think of how many frequency waves are passing right by you, right now. You can't see the WIFI waves traversing your living room, but you know they are there when you go online. I believe sasquatch can raise their frequency to a level above where our eye can detect them. It obviously takes power to do that. Is that why they are seen in broad daylight at the Montana vortex? Are they charging up while they charge through?

Octopi and chameleon can manipulate their color. They can change the emitting frequency of color on the surface of their bodies. I believe sasquatch might be able to go even further and raise the frequency of their whole body.

It also could explain why I couldn't see whatever walked up beside me that night when I was attempting to record UFO's. I had my camera on the Infrared light setting, which is a lower frequency than visible light. I'm thinking he was vibrating above visible light and therefore invisible to me and my I.R. camera.

What I do struggle to explain is how that sasquatch in the House of Mystery turned into a bright light, then a white mist, disappearing while appearing to float up and vanish? Also, if my cloaker was just vibrating at a higher frequency than visible light, like a chameleon, wouldn't his mass block my view of the landscape beyond his body? That is why I believe they can raise the frequency of their whole body and not just their surface, becoming transparent like radio waves.

Early in 2020 I came across some prints that looked suspicious. They weren't well defined, but I interpreted three different sizes of prints. It appeared to be an adult sasquatch with two juveniles. I might add that this is just a few miles away from where my great nephew Mason and I had the visit from juveniles and an adult to the perimeter of our camp in July of 2019.

In fact, the area where I found the prints is in the general direction they left after they performed their antics for Mason and I on that late July afternoon. The last thing we heard after going to bed was the adult male call back to us. I began to poke around in that direction to see what I could find? I figured if I got close enough, they would let me know somehow? Were those prints an indication that I had found the area they had been attempting to guide me to?

On my first search in that direction, I ended up on a landing in a clear-cut. This area overlooked the Willapa valley and beyond. It was a magnificent and beautiful sight. I was standing there admiring the view when I heard a sasquatch call from just a few hundred yards away to the northwest. It was a very loud and unusual call. It actually gave me a little chill. He began with a call starting low and then going high with a wild crescendo, then went into some other vocal manipulations. It was one of the wildest calls I've heard out there. Because of the similarity in style to the call Mason and I heard the night of our July encampment, I was pretty sure it was the same sasquatch.

Then, about three minutes later, I heard another call from way further to the northwest. I decided they were attempting to refine my search and were actually guiding me back toward the direction where we camped in July.

I sent them a telepathic thank you, got back into my vehicle and began driving in that direction. Before long I came across a fresh break of a branch on a tree next to the road. That was about where I heard the first call. I knew the second call was where I needed to go. Below is an example of a double break.

I spent a few trips kicking around and looking for a sign? I did find some interesting stuff in that direction, including scat full of apples. I felt the scat belonged to them and not a bear. I could see bear scat nearby and it was black from eating cascara berries. The apple scat looked human, except the piles were enormous and there were several of them. They were as big as a basketball cut in half. It would have taken several bears to make all of them and they didn't look like bear.

Kicking around up in the woods, in the same general area as the apple tree, I found two more huge piles. Those were placed near the beginning of two different abandoned log roads leading up a hill, perhaps showing me the way to go? They do not have the same sensibilities toward scat as we would, by the way.

On Labor Day weekend 2019, I again went solo out into that area. I drove to a landing in the middle of a clear-cut and hung around. It was a very nice, warm day and I was enjoying playing my guitar. After a while I got up and began to move toward the driver side of the Subaru to get something. As I walked toward the door, I was looking at the trees that were about a hundred yards away and one of them fell over!

I immediately switched out of my flip flops into my hiking boots and began to make my way up to where I saw the tree go down. There was a lot of tree fall in that area and it was difficult to traverse. I couldn't tell which tree they had pushed down, if indeed they had pushed it down? While I was searching, I thought I heard a female voice up a draw from where I was. There was no chance it was a human because of the location, so I figured they probably pushed the tree down.

About a half hour after and several hundred yards to the northwest, I again heard a huge tree go down. I heard it crack and then smash to the ground a few seconds later. They were showing me the direction again, trying to help me refine my search. Also, confirming to me that they had pushed the first tree down. Eventually, that led to where I found the prints.

After finding the prints I took a look around and found an enchanting, isolated meadow. It was flooded by the creek that runs through it. I was struck by the beauty of the area and the prints and decided to investigate further.

I went on Google Earth and took a look at the area. I could see there was a waterfall not far from the meadow. I went back and tried to find a way to the waterfall, but the water was still too high. On my way back to my car I crossed a small creek and a disturbance in the water caught my eye. I thought a fish had hit the surface of the crystal-clear, smooth water and I was determined to find it?

As I was looking for the fish other disturbances showed up on the water's surface. There was no wind and no fish. The water was crystal clear and it was easy to see that there was nothing to account for the disturbance, such as a methane leak or spring from below. What was making the water act like that? I recorded the event on my phone and decided to return to observe, examine and contemplate the question more?

A couple of days later I returned to find the water was completely undisturbed and in fact, as smooth as a mirror. There also was a newly fallen tree down across the creek at that location. The weather had been calm and beautiful for the few days that had transpired before I got the opportunity to return. Why did the tree fall?

What do I make of this? I believe they might have been showing me the location of a ley line. There was definitely some electromagnetic force at work there? Water is a semiconductor and that is what they utilized for a medium. They pushed that tree down as a way of autographing their work. It was their way of letting me know that they were there and responsible for the demonstration.

Like a light wave, I could not see the ley line or demarcation line without the water acting as a medium to inform me.

I have never attempted to divine anything in my life, but I plan to attempt to divine this creek and the other power points I know about. I am going to turn a couple of my metal coat hangers into a couple of divining rods. I also have some copper tubing I'm going to convert.

CHAPTER 12

What is Going On?

I CAN'T GUARANTEE I have all or most of the answers? I have very few, in fact. I'm guessing I'm just beginning my journey into the metaphysical? It is hard to imagine what will come next? Every year I believe they couldn't possibly top the year before and every year I'm wrong. I still have the number 111 flashing in front of my face daily, so I'm thinking this isn't over. There is more to learn.

Then again, I could be wrong and this book could be the culmination of my part in the mission? I don't believe it will be the end of my friendship with my special family, one way or the other.

I do have a theory or two I have formed and reformed over the last few years. My current theories are based on what I've experienced and what I've learned through study on all pertinent subjects. Much of those studies I was guided to, one way or the other. I consider them my current theories because they can change on a dime and have a few times when presented with some alternate evidence. I don't ever want to be stuck in a box. Almost on a daily basis I am utilizing meta cognition to keep checking for possible erroneous conclusions.

One of the things I look for are consistencies in eye witness reports. Eye witness reports are very important in giving me a hint as to what direction to consider for answers. For example, many of the people I know, both in person and in closed sasquatch groups, receive gifts that are blue. Balloons are favorites of theirs for giving. I've received at least three balloons and other blue items, as well. These blue gifts appear for experiencers all across American continent. By America, I mean Canada too.

In the spring of 2020, I replied to an open question on a closed sasquatch Face Book site. The questioner was asking about blue balloons? I commented that I'd received a few balloons and knew others all across the continent that had also received the, something blue gift. Often that blue gift is a balloon.

Then next morning, after posting a comment on blue balloons I went on a hike past a small waterfall. I'd personally decided to call those falls, Shaman Falls, about three years ago. A day after naming the falls I went hiking past it and there was a blue balloon stuck in a tree above the falls. I'm sure they were listening to me as I conducted my ceremony and approved of my naming. https://youtu.be/2OOwqXpUMtA

Where do they get the balloons? So far this year I've seen two loose balloons float right down the street past my house as they slowly gained altitude and headed for the forest. One of those was blue. Obviously, someone was having a celebration of some sort down the street. IT's A BOY!?

The day after responding to that man's open question on Face Book I hiked past Shaman falls again and that made me think of the blue balloon that appeared mysteriously the next day above those falls.

I hiked up to a landing where I can see down the beautiful Smith creek valley and then began to hike back out. On the hike out is when I saw the balloon in the middle of my path, not far from Shaman Falls. It wasn't there on the way out and there was no wind blowing. Besides, it was deflated, so it didn't float there. They were obviously listening to my thoughts. Below is the balloon and Shaman falls.

It's just an old worn-out Mylar balloon, but I consider it a very special gift and it is hanging in a corner of my living room. Also, it has stars on it!

Someone once told me their communication system is like the internet. They can dial into my site and listen in or watch, or they can tune me out. Perhaps there is some kind of notice signal when I come into their area and then they tune in and see what I'm up to? I'm fairly certain sasquatch always know when I'm out there and my location. I also don't believe they are the only ones dialing into me? ET is on that communication network too and I believe they are more consistent listeners. This is all conjecture, of course.

What does the blue represent? It is the color of a higher frequency wave. Perhaps, it is symbolic of their ability to cloak and traverse dimensions or parallel universes? I've also read that blue is a healing color.

My sister Teri was in for her last check up to see if she was cancer free in the year 2011? They anesthetized her for the procedure. While she was under, she dreamt of a blue dragon hovering above her before it morphed into a dolphin and swam away. She sensed the dragon was sending her a message, telling her she was healed and would be okay. That turned out to be the outcome. She has been cancer free to this day.

In fact, I just realized as I was writing this, her procedure was just a few weeks before my first, recognized encounter with a sasquatch. The one where I smelled that strong odor.

When she told me about her dream, I was still a skeptic/atheist and my thought was that her own subconscious was trying to ease her anxiety. No way did I believe she had received a visit from benevolent spirits or guardian angels. Now of course, I believe it was a visit from some kind of spirit, or what some might call, an angel. Maybe they even were responsible for part or most of her recovery? The first prognosis gave her only a 5% chance of survival.

I've known many people who claim healing from both sasquatch and ET's. A few of them were miraculous recoveries from ailments that were so grave the doctor gave them a virtual death sentence.

These people are sincere and many of their stories are consistent, sometimes with a twist I had never considered before. For instance, one young lady told me ET healed her, but she doesn't want anything to do with them. She was very frightened of the whole thing, feeling a bit like a trapped animal. She said she was born into a family of abductees and in fact I talked to her father and mother who supported her claim.

To me it seems strange to be afraid of the beings who healed you. But, as far as I can remember I've never been in her situation, so it's easy for me to say. I think that we have made it more frightening with our culture of denial. We deny that anything beyond our accepted reality could possibly exist and therefore, when we encounter them, our whole psyche is put under attack. An encounter with high strangeness that lies too far outside the realm of how we perceive reality can be shocking and terrifically disorienting.

Another acquaintance told me he woke up in an extraterrestrial vehicle during a healing. He had eye contact with the ET healer and asked if he could have a tour of the ship when they were done? He said the ET just looked at him, smiled, touched him and he was out. That man said he even had dental work done once where they fixed his aching tooth and filled it. I asked him what they filled it with? He didn't know, but I could tell he was intrigued by the question and maybe thinking of a way to find out?

Some of my acquaintances and friends would claim to only having contact with sasquatch. Others are alien abductees, involved with the sasquatch phenomena as well. I even know a couple who have matching scars where their implants are. One of them tried to dig his out and almost got a hold of it when it suddenly moved, forcing him to give up.

I don't have a memory of any abduction, but at a UFO summit I had a place on my head checked for an implant. I had suspected that area of my head soon after I began seeing the UFO's. The checker said it was registering something on his instrument? I've tried to dig mine out at least three times. The last time, I really dug in earnest leaving my head a bloody mess. I failed and decided never to try again.

I've seen implants in displays presented by Darrel Simms, the UFO Hunter, as he is called. By the way, Darrel Simms is an abductee and yes, I state that as if it is fact. I believe it is fact. I believe most, if not all of these people who have told me their abduction stories are telling the truth.

In one of Darrel's books about implants there is speculation that they can see through the experiencer's eyes. This is possible if the implant is connected to the nervous system, which it appears to be. I know they are paying very close attention to me. Even more so than I had ever imagined. They have proven that through electronic manipulation on a few occasions.

I've also studied ancient history, science, archeology, math, geometry, physics, ufology, cryptozoology, clairvoyance, telepathy, remote viewing, mythology, religion, sacred math, field theory and so on…All of these subjects I find very interesting and I devoted as much of my spare time as I could to my studies. They have helped me make some sense of this strange world as I explore it. The thing is, the deeper I go down that rabbit hole the stranger it gets. But, I'm good with that. In fact, I like it. I am driven by my overwhelming compulsion to know and understand as much as I can before my time is up. By the way, I now believe death is an illusion.

One of the big questions I'd like to know the answer to is when did they choose me? Because, I've received the message that I was "chosen". One sensitive told me that I was chosen because they felt I had a personality they could work with. I'd love to know how they came to that conclusion? What was the vetting process? Did I subconsciously apply for the position? Possibly? Once upon a time, around 1980, I was in such a sorry emotional state I reached out to the universe and asked if there was a place for me? It was soon after that when the strange began to happen.

Although there are other clues that I might have been chosen from birth. Those clues I'm not going to share at this time, mainly because I haven't had time to explore and list all them.

The effort that has gone into my teachings and the elaborate setting up of this, whatever it is, indicates that it is very important. There are so many elements that are synchronized in a well-planned, timely orchestrated dance. After all, I'm not the only one who was "chosen" for this. There are, at least, half a dozen or more.

Jill Smith, for instance, purchased her property when I was in the right frame of mind and possessed enough information to consider looking on Google earth and determine, as she told me, it was meant for her. After checking the location and distance of 36 miles, I knew it was also meant for me to visit that powerful place.

Something that really puzzles me is how very important I appear to be to them? They show me not only love, but so much devotion. I've set out overnight recorders and more than once I've heard an exhale from, who I presume is my designated guard for the night? They also seem to go way out of their way to say "hello". That is why I've had so much contact. All I have to do is go out and camp somewhere. If I stay long enough, anywhere, they will come if it is possible and most of the time it is. It makes me wonder?

I feel a heavy responsibility to them. As if this is my duty, beyond it being a passion. They have given me so much. I live the most interesting life there is. I'm a curious cat and they are scratching my itch. I feel obligated to repay their devotion. I'm not just talking about sasquatch, but ET and maybe spirits too.

Out of the blue a sensitive, who I met at a UFO summit, emailed me and said she had received a message, "Russell is a sasquatch in human form." She asked if that could be true!? I emailed back and told her I was pretty sure it was honorary. But, am I sure? Not really.

One of my friends was born awoke, meaning she can remember all of her past lives. Soon after meeting her, things began to get weird. I felt somehow that I knew her, even though I could not possibly have met her.

I also felt we were meant to know each other. I'd had a premonition that I was going to meet a special young lady a year or two before. Then, just before we met, I dreamt of the circumstances of our meeting which ultimately came true. We have become very close friends and it is very natural and familiar.

I do not know what part she plays? She immediately struck me as being an old soul, though she is forty-five years my junior. Knowing that I am not going to live forever, I wonder if she is the one to take the baton forward? After all, the best I can do at this juncture is a bit of directed conjecture? I'm not done living life, yet it's taken a few years to get to this point and I'm not going to live forever. I am in pretty good shape for a dinosaur, though. Hopefully, I'll have a few more years to piece more of this puzzle together? I also hope she will outlive me, by a long shot. I send her short updates on line of what I've experienced and learned. She is a highly intelligent, compassionate and an eager student. I have complete confidence in her.

She has also dreamt of sasquatch on a couple of occasions. She said in her dream she can't quite see them. She knows they are a family and that I'm supposed to take her out and introduce her. I am really looking forward to that.

I'd use her name, but she has a budding career in the entertainment industry and I believe it would be best for her to remain unnamed until she has established herself. Who knows, it could be thirty years before she gets another tap on the shoulder and it becomes her turn?

This mission is, at least, forty-five years in the making and if you count the famous P/G film it goes back over fifty years to 1967. I believe that may have been a purposeful reveal and might have been part of this project? A virtual tap on the shoulder to humanity, as it were. It has amazed me how they fine-tuned everything to fit. The math, for instance, is too coincidental. There is just too much to be a lucky roll of the dice several times in a row.

I have four pyramids in my living room, which have been there for years. My friend, Russell Wilson gave me a large beautiful marble one, which stands about six inches high and is heavy. I now keep it aligned, with a broad face to magnetic north. I do that because it increases it power, according to Nick Nelson and I believe him. He has done experiments on these things and strikes me as a very honest and earnest gentleman. Besides, I was given a message in the form of a disappearing bear to believe this man.

He isn't the only one who believes in "pyramid power", a seventies, hippy fad that was once winked at and chuckled over. I remember laughing at it myself. Ken Wheeler explains its power using a fire hose analogy. Just like the nozzle of a fire hose narrowing at the end increases the velocity of the water going out of it, a pyramid shaped magnet acts the same way. Ken can demonstrate this by utilizing a ferro cell to show the magnetic fields of a pyramidal magnet. Nick Nelson is another genius that discovered pyramid power through his experiments. Some believe the great pyramid was built on top of a vortex field. Could it have created a vortex field when built? Increased electromagnetism has been detected at the apex of the pyramid. It could be that power is generated by the pyramid itself purely because of its geometric shape?

I now know there is a connection to the Giza Pyramid. There are too many numerical coincidences for that not to be true. Did you know that if you enlarged the Great Pyramid by 43,200 (432) times it would almost fit perfectly within the hollowed out northern hemisphere of our globe? With the four corners of its base touching the edge of the equator, it would only be 11 miles shy of touching the north pole.

If you draw a line with a 20-degree eastern declination from true north starting at the Oregon vortex and going north, it will eventually end up at the Great Pyramid. Did that happen by chance? Did all of the numbers line up by chance? I don't know how an objective mind could come to that conclusion? The odds of everything I've sighted in this book being coincidence is beyond reasonable. The principle of Occom's razor does apply here and the simplest answer is that there was a creator of some sort? Who?

How smart is sasquatch? I believe they are probably more intelligent than us. I base that on the fact that they have a bee hive brain. I came across an experiment where they were connecting two people with electrodes to their brains. When two people are connected in such a way it increases their ability to solve puzzles. This occurs even when one of the participants is not solving the puzzle and just sitting passively, doing nothing. All sasquatch are connected to each other and therefore their collective brain power is substantial. Their network is like a powerful computer array, an organic interferometer.

I began asking questions of my teacher in the form of glyphs. I first put a triangle of rocks out and sent the message, "What do you have to say about the Great pyramid?" It took a few days and I received the answer in the form of a white crystal placed, as if it was floating above the pyramid.

After receiving this crystal, I placed it in the hands of a few sensitives and asked them what they could tell me about it? One told me that it represented a member of an ancient civilization coming through a portal. Could that be true? Could a portal form above the pyramid when it is operational? She also said "Trust your teacher." I did not mention to her that I had a teacher.

I suppose I over utilize my meta-cognition at times and that was the why I received the message, "Trust your teacher." But it is a natural way for my brain to work, so my teacher is just going to have to put up with it. As I wrote those words in the previous sentence, I could see my teacher roll his eyes in my mind's eye.

At the top of the first picture is the crystal.

One of my big questions is when were the vortex fields that pepper the western U.S. and the continent at large formed or placed? Nick Nelson says it might be that the mere building of the Giza pyramids created the vortex fields on the other side of the world? I like that theory, but I'm not completely sold on it.

If you consider where Orion's belt rose on the summer solstice 12,500 years ago as viewed from the Giza complex, you might conclude that is when the Great pyramid was probably built? Since so much of this information has to do with astrological alignments why wouldn't you conclude that? The three main pyramids are in the form of Orion's belt, for goodness sakes.

Scientists have done carbon 14 analysis inside the great pyramid and it indicated the organic material they analyzed was less than six thousand years old. However, that organic material might have been left by a grave robber? In my mind that is interesting evidence, but only one piece of a puzzle that has a lot of other puzzle pieces pointing to a possible alternative direction.

I've also read an historical account written on papyrus by a man who transported large blocks down the Nile River to the Giza complex. The local Egyptologists claim he was transporting building materials for the great pyramid. How can they claim, without evidence, that man was transporting huge blocks for the Great pyramid? There are other pyramids close by. They ignore any evidence that points toward a much more ancient origin of the Great pyramid. Also, there is a total of 153 pyramids at the Giza complex without any sign of being built as tombs. I believe that most Egyptologists are earnest, yet stuck in their own box.

There are geographical accommodations made for vortex fields. The Rogue River, for instance takes an identical, mirror turn, while passing by the Oregon vortex. In other words, there appears to be areas of topography that have morphed due to these vortex fields. Geological changes take place over millions of years, yet the Montana vortex fields are configured in the same pattern as Orion's belt and the western commercial vortex fields are in the form of the constellation Orion. So, how did topographical changes occur, conforming with the vortex fields over millions of years before the constellation of Orion was even in its current configuration, as viewed from earth? I am at a loss?

It could be the pyramid itself was created by an ancient civilization to enhance the power of those vortex fields. When it was operational that might have afforded easy access back and forth through portals connected from the great pyramid to other worlds?

The pyramid itself has a large room below its base. Once upon a time that room, which they aptly named Harmony, might have been filled with water. There are also aqueducts of running water under the Great Pyramid that are still active today. Water is a semi-conductor and might have served to enhance the great pyramids power? Did that water vibrate at certain frequencies, enhancing the power of the Great Pyramid, opening up portals to other worlds? Was the pyramid a power station, perhaps created to strengthen portals connecting alien worlds to ours?

You might wonder why ETs are hiding from humanity? In, at least, three historical texts, witnesses have seen battles going on in the air between alien adversaries. There was one in Nuremberg Germany in 1561. Then another in 1566 in Switzerland. Back then they didn't have a local paper, they had wood carvings and a town crier. The wood carvings that reported and recorded those incidences still exist today and have illustrations of round, elongated and ex shaped craft doing battle over those cities. It is documented eye witness testimony of battles between two airborne foes of unknown origin.

Not all is good with the universe. There are factions out there and they are also here. The Sumerians talk about the Anunnaki, which according to some translators means children of heaven and earth, or those from the heavens came, or of royal blood. The earliest texts to mention them date back 6,500 + years. In other words, way back to the earliest known written records. The Sumerians worshipped and served the Anunnaki. They also claim these "gods" gifted mankind with math we still use today. For instance, our division of time into 60 minutes and 60 seconds. The Sumerians utilized a 60 base math system. The worldwide matrix, according to Carl Munck, utilizes a ten-base system. Could that be an accommodation for our modern use of the base ten system, or is it a universally utilized mathematical base?

I used to ponder why we in the U.S. were stuck with inches, feet and miles when almost everyone else in the world had converted to the metric system? I wondered why we were so slow and backward and still utilizing such an outdated system? I now believe it was necessary for us to retain that system in order for us to recognize the road signs that were placed for us. Also, after review, I see the advantages of that ancient metrology. All of these monuments and vortices seem to be built utilizing this ancient system of measurement, which predates recorded history. If the U.S. had converted to the metric system, we may not have noticed all of these synchronicities? In other words, we were guided subconsciously to not convert to the metric system in order to facilitate the eventual reveal. It appears, it might be a more universal system.

Next, I left an open question with a glyph in the form of the constellation Orion? Again, it took a few days and then three parallel sticks showed up in what would be the head position of the constellation. Above those three parallel sticks was an ex made with two sticks. The symbol ex is generally believed to mean friend or family within the sasquatch research community. Also, I wondered about the three sticks and if they relate somehow to the 111 that keeps flashing in front of my face? I got a feeling they do. I'm thinking they might represent a portal for transportation? My impression is that the number 111 is important in some way for portals?

Look carefully at the bottom of the ex and you will see the three sticks.

There were ancient civilizations that believed we've been visited by beings from Orion, the Pleiades, Cygnus, or Sirius. The Pleiades, otherwise known as the seven sisters, is a cluster made up of over three hundred stars. I would imagine there is a lot of life there?

It would be foolish to think that all ETs are kind, compassionate beings. In fact, I believe there is an underground struggle going on here on earth, right now. There are those aligned with good intentions and those nefarious beings who want to enslave us.

Recently, I saw a Mexican artifact in a private collection that had artwork on it depicting one man worshiping and another paying tribute to a large being sitting on a throne. There was also a perfect representation of a flying saucer floating above that ruling being. I've seen something very similar in Sumerian artwork dating back thousands of years. The Mexican artifact had some glue on it which provided organic material that could be carbon 14 dated. It dated back 9,400 years!

If you take these artifacts seriously, there were extraterrestrial rulers on earth in the distant past that ruled openly. What happened to them? In an ancient Mayan myth, the extraterrestrial ruler named Ra was dethroned by another ET named Wata. Did Ra then go to Egypt and become their sun God?

I believe it is very possible that the descriptions of floods in many myths among ancient civilizations and the bible, might have been to displace or kill these rulers resulting in human collateral damage.

Puma Punku, in Bolivia, was built with precise instrumentation. Experts marvel at the precise inside cuts on stone, which is an extremely hard and difficult material to work with. The blocks appear to have been manufactured as if they had been created at a factory. They now lay in ruins, scattered around, some half buried as if subject to a cataclysmic flood.

Uphill from that location, over twelve thousand years ago, was a massive glacier. I've heard it speculated that a meteor hit the glacier causing a massive melt and run off that flooded Puma Punku and left it in its current disarray?

Around that time a huge ice dam up in Canada held back an enormous volume of water several times more than all the great lakes. Some say a large meteor was responsible for breaking that dam, which resulted in the final demise of the large North American fauna, such as the sabretooth tiger and mammoth. When that dam broke it raised the Mediterranean Sea by over thirty feet in a matter of a few hours. That caused a land bridge separating the Black Sea area from the Mediterranean to rupture and flood thousands of square miles of terrain where the Black Sea is now located. There are many ancient settlements that got flooded simultaneously in the valley that are now under water of the Black Sea. An eye witness from that time would consider it a worldwide flood, because to them, it would seem to be their whole world had flooded.

Cataclysmic floods are spoken about in many ancient texts and oral traditions. Were these floods directed to wipe out the world-wide ET ruling class of that era? That might have put an end to the overt ruling, subjugation and enslavement of the human race? Now everything is subtle and underground so to speak, or, maybe it actually is underground?

I believe there is a struggle going on right now between these factions. One side are our protectors and want to help us evolve both spiritually and physically. The other side wants us to devolve into a malleable population of slaves. Perhaps, they both have competing genetic manipulation programs? Perhaps there are more than two sides in the competition? What I have done is pick a side. I believe it is the side of compassion, love and justice.

Why do we reject metaphysics? The guy behind the pulpit hasn't a lot of power if an individual can gain knowledge, consult spirits and the universe through the use of metaphysics on their own. Metaphysical understanding threatens the power structure of instituted religion. Therefore, make the population reject metaphysics to the point of characterizing it as either myth or the devil.

Metaphysics was made illegal back in the late 300s by the Roman ruler, Theodosius and it stuck with great effect. That is why so many in our so-called modern world reject the idea of ghosts, UFO's, sasquatch and everything that is associated with the metaphysical.

I know extraterrestrials are here and actively participating in our world. Logically, I have to conclude that we would be slaves if not for being protected by compassionate, brave and spiritual beings. If you believe the ancient historical accounts of past civilizations, then you would have to agree we've been ruled over before by some bad players.

They would rule us now if they were allowed to stick their heads above ground, or water.

I know that I've been unconsciously guided several times in my life, for instance to buy my house. Why wouldn't these various factions have the power to influence world affairs by influencing our leaders? A subtle push here and there can make a huge impact on world political dynamics. Who knows, maybe they even release a targeted virus to do some specific culling or social adjustment of some sort? How? Perhaps all it took was for an epidemiologist to be guided to make a small, subconscious mistake in the handling of a bat or vial containing the virus?

Don't get me wrong, I'm not much for conspiracy theories. I consider 99% of them to be total bunk. I do wonder, though? There is definitely something going on and that something has been going on for a long time.

I received two messages the last time I was at a summit. The first one was "Courage, courage, courage". The second one was "Finish your book, finish your book, finish your book."

I'm hoping the first message, which is about courage, is only referring to the flack I will get from those who will believe I made this all up? I can deal with that. The second message? I've finished, with only two more sentences to go.

What's next for me? I have no idea, but I have a feeling it is going to be amazing; it always is.

The end

www.ingramcontent.com/pod-product-compliance
Lightning Source LLC
Chambersburg PA
CBHW061201070526
44579CB00009B/82